Ethical Response to Corruption

By the Same Author

– Ethical and Human Values in Medical Science

About the Author

Dr. Niru Hazarika, former Dean Faculty of Arts, Gauhati University and Former Memebr of ICSSR, New Delhi served Gauhati University as teacher of Political Science for more than three decades. She started her service career as teacher in Political Science of Gauhati University and ended her career in it. She was also a student of this University.

She is the first lady in Northeast India to be awarded the degree of D.Litt. Under her guidance 60 students from various professions have been awarded the degree of Doctor of Philosophy till date. Her specialization is in public administration, Government and Politics in Northeast India and Human Rights.

Dr. Hazarika authored and Co-authored several books. Her same significant works are Public Service Commissions in India, Ethnic Autonomy in Northeast India: A Search for an Answer, Insurgency and Beyond, A Century of Civil Service in Northeast India etc. She co-authored Local-Self Government in India, Government and Politics in Northeast India (Three volumes etc.)

She attended several international conferences and seminars and visited USA, UK, France, Holland, Spain etc. on academic programmes. She published articles in several national and international journals.

Ethical Response to Corruption

Niru Hazarika

CONCEPT PUBLISHING COMPANY PVT. LTD.
NEW DELHI-110059

ISBN-13: 978-93-88937-59-7

First Published 2020

Published and Printed by

Concept
Since 1974

Concept Publishing Company Pvt. Ltd.
A/15-16, Commercial Block, Mohan Garden
New Delhi-110059 (INDIA)
T: 91 11 25351460, 91 11 25351794
E: publishing@conceptpub.com; *W*: www.conceptpub.com

Cataloging in Publication Data--Courtesy: D.K. Agencies (P) Ltd. <docinfo@dkagencies.com>

Hazarika, Niru, 1947- author.
Ethical response to corruption / Niru Hazarika.
pages cm
Includes bibliographical references and index.
ISBN 9789388937597

1. Corruption—Moral and ethical aspects—India. 2. Corruption—India—Prevention. I. Title.

LCC HV6771.I4H39 2020 | DDC 364.13230954 23

Presented to

Dr. Dhrubajyoti Bhaumik

Former Professor of Political Science
Dean of Faculty of Arts, Commerce & Law
Director, Centre for Women's Studies
North Bengal University

With High Appreciation for his dedication and contribution to the academic world

Preface

One of the oldest civilizations was born in India. This country had a highly developed human culture to which the leaders of the major religions of the world, social reformers and the rulers of different old kingdoms of the country made significant contributions. The British penetration of the subcontinent in the form of East India Company and afterwards establishment of the British Raj under the rule of the Bitish Crown had distorted the human aspect of the Indian culture.

However, the liberation movement under the leadership of Mahatma Gandhi provided enough scope to rebuild the moral or human foundation of the social culture of India. Gandhi was a great moral leader and his life itself was a storehouse of bricks and mortars in the form of truth and non-violence, for repairing and rebuilding the human culture of the country.

The framers of the Constitution of India took utmost care to sustain the human aspect of the social culture while framing the Constitution. It is reflected very well in the Preamble to the Constitution itself. It emphasized the need to secure justice, liberty, equality and fraternity amongst all sections of the people for very survival of Indian democracy. Democracy, as a way of life, is the only device to construct a path on which all of us irrespective of caste, religion, language, place of birth or in short as human beings, can walk together to reach our destination.

Unfortunately, the people of India have failed to realize in-depth philosophy of Indian democracy mirrored in the Preamble to the Constitution. Gradually, space for ethical and human values has been narrowed down in Indian democracy. Political democracy finds space in the system of election only. This system is also surviving only in a degenerated form. With the progress of science and technology life has become comfortable and here begins the process of dehumanization of the Indian democracy. Man has failed to generate human power in him resulting space for the emergence of money and muscle power. Naturally, the infrastructure (consisting of love, affection, fellow feeling, caring and sharing of views or ideas, safeguarding of human rights and dignity etc.) for development of a human society has been totally distorted. The existing Indian society is suffering from ethical crisis.

John F. Kennedy, in his message to Congress on 27 April, 1961 (referred by Carol W. Lewis in his writing on Ethics Codes and Ethics Agencies: Current Practices and Emerging Trends) said, "The ultimate answer to ethical problems in government is honest people in a good ethical environment. No web of statute or regulation, however intricately conceived, can hope to deal with the myriad possible challenges to a man's integrity or his devotion to the public interest.

Nevertheless formal regulation is required – regulations which can lay down clear guidelines of policy, punish venality and double-dealing, and set a general ethical tone for the conduct of public business.

Criminal statutes or presidential orders, no matter how carefully conceived or meticulously drafted, cannot hope to deal effectively with every problem of ethical behaviour or conflict of interest. Problems arise in infinite variation. They often involve subtle and difficult judgments...And even the best of statutes or regulations will fail of their purpose if they are not vigorously and wisely administered."

The book is an attempt to rethink loudly that our problem is not with our destination, our problem is to construct the right path to the destination. Time has come to realize that as a builder of the nation one has to depend on human power, neither money nor muscle power can lead the human power, it is in the other way round.

I am extremely grateful to all the authors/thinkers/reformers whose writings/speeches strengthen my faith on ethical and human values as strong weapons to eradicate the ailments of the global human society and this strength induces me conceptualize this book, 'Ethical Response to Corruption'.

I must express my gratefulness to Mr. A.K. Mittal and the editorial Board for their kind cooperation to materialize my thought in the form of a book.

Niru Hazarika

Contents

Introduction

Human society is changeable and in the face of it the governance of a state must be dynamic and innovative to maintain its efficiency. The dynamism and innovation features of governance demand intervention in the way of life of the people to keep pace of progress of a society. The scholars coin it as "Developmental Intervention." This concept may be considered as another valuable addition to the administrative process of a democratic country.

Here the notable point is that the developmental process may cause inconveniences in several ways to the people as well as to the administrators. First, development administration is possible only with administrative development; second, people have to move from conservatism to dynamism in spite of all the inconveniences caused by this intervention. Perseverance, tolerance, acceptance of truth, realization of human values, mutual respect for each other etc. are the bricks and mortars to build the path of progress along with other physical framework. It is also a difficult task, though not impossible. It is true in case of both the ruler and the ruled. They must be highly sensitive to human values and moral context of their actions.

The dynamism and moral aspect of public administration are well projected by Robert B. Denhardt when he said—public administration is concerned with managing change in pursuit of publicly defined societal values. Since 1970s the scholars are rethinking the state of the relationship between politics and administration. Along with it there is the urgent need of having a fresh look to the administration and people relationship also. Democratic governance in today's fast changing global society is about much more than the right to vote and mere welfare of the people.

In the language of Seyed Mohmmad Khatami, the global community ultimately requires the emergence of a responsive moral society, avoiding the use of force and coercion in national and international disputes. Values and norms that are not codified into laws, and laws that lack enforcement mechanisms, will have no tangible effect. Thus globalization is intertwined with the articulation of new collective rights and ethics, and the ensuing impact on national and international norms and institutions.

It is felt that the space for humanity in the global society has been narrowed down to a great extent by various inhuman activities in different parts of the world. It is a serious threat to modern democracy. Disappearance of human power, emergence of unethical behaviour, domination of money power, activism of irrational elements of man, strong arguments in favour of undemocratic behaviour of leaders, unresponsiveness to public needs and aspirations, lack of integration between word, work and thought of modern man, disregard to human dignity and violation of human rights at every stage of man's life etc. are the very prominent indicators of degeneration of democratic principles across the world. It is no denying the fact that honesty, integrity and humanity have been thrown out mercilessly from the modern society. Very soon the nations of the world have forgotten the situations leading to establishment of League of Nations and United Nations of Organization followed by various other Organizations at the international and national levels as the saviors of humanity from the scourge of unthinkable barbarity.

India's advancement in the field of science and technology is highly appreciable. It expedites the journey of traditional India to the world of modernization and it also provides comfort to man's life to a great extent. This is a journey for more than seventy years. In this journey we have failed to sustain our human power as leading force of life. Gradually, human power becomes fragile. Human value fails to work as torch bearer in the journey. Surprisingly, during this period the impact of India's freedom struggle under the leadership of Mahatma Gandhi and sacrifice of lives of people, ideals adhered by eminent Indian thinkers who participated in the movement have disappeared from the country. Both the rulers and the ruled started adopting easy way to be modernized. We have become imitators. Naturally, corruption in various forms has taken place in the administrative system. In the beginning it was confined to certain limited areas of governance, but gradually it infects every phase of governance. Now, it has become the way of life to both the rulers and the ruled.

What is needed today is that the modern Indians have to visit our past to X-ray those values in the perspective of their relevance in the modern Indian democracy and to utilize those values which are found necessary for strengthening our path to democratic way of life.

While attempting to climb up in the escalator of progress with the perspectives of modernization and development of science and technology there is the possibility of absorption of many unwelcome or destructive elements by the society due to lack of far-sightedness. We are depending on superficial knowledge about those scientific innovations. In the similar way we have rejected several social customs or social habits required for revitalizing our existing nation. Here lies the significance of the reasoning power of a man to judge what is to be accepted and what is to be rejected to sustain our democratic way of life and to walk smoothly on the path of progress.

While talking about the responsibility of the rulers in a democracy people's responsibility cannot be ignored to make democratic government successful in rendering service to the people. Maximum use of human power of the people is the key for creation of a democratic society which in turn becomes fertile soil for strengthening democratic ideals with wide coverage of the society.

The serious threat to democracy in India is the scourge of corruption. Despite having the vigilant press, an outspoken civil society and an impartial judiciary, the most disheartening fact of Indian democracy is corruption. It continues to exist in both covert and overt ways at all levels of politics, bureaucracy and private life. It is a serious obstacle to good governance. Both the rulers and the ruled have to make serious efforts to eradicate it. Ethical response to corruption may be one of these efforts.

I
Corruption

Introduction: Corruption is emerging as irrepressible challenge to democracy across the world of today. It is distorting all the regional, national and international norms of ethics and human values which constitute the basic foundation of modern democracy. Almost all the developing countries are badly affected by it. India may be the worst victim of this deadly disease.

Corruption causes not only economic distortion, it distorts the whole concept of democracy for which most countries of the world fought at the heavy cost of man and material for many years. In the contemporary political world of India corruption has already undermined the legitimacy of the government with the loss of public trust in the government. The protest movements against the decisions of the Governments launched by different sections of the people reflect it very clearly. The erosion of efficiency and humaneness of almost all the public organizations has come to surface very prominently.

Moral standards in public service are severely affected by corruption. It is an obstruction to development; it affects stability of peace and security of a nation. It also erodes public trust and confidence. Besides, corruption causes lack of quality in essential services, poor management of public resources. It exploits the poor and innocent people, violate human rights and ignores human values.

It is very surprising experience that in contemporary India corruption has become a white-colour crime and the involvement in corruption is no longer a covert activity. The corrupt persons who are in white-colour job are involved in these unethical activities overtly. They also pick up the techniques of defending their unethical activities by various kinds of mischievous means. This situation proves that of all the animals man is expert in hiding his wickedness. The ethical vacuity in the politico-administrative world of India warns us that we are retreating fast to the state of nature as described by English political thinker, Thomas Hobbes.

Immediately after independence of India top priority was given to economic development of the country. Due care was not taken to the development of human resources. In addition to this, involvement of the poor people in unethical or corrupt practices was handled with humanitarian attitude for various reasons. It was opined that economic poverty was one of the major causes of these corrupt or unethical activities. In course of time, it is noticed that corruption has become white-colour crime in most cases and poor people are involved in these corrupt activities, knowingly or unknowingly under the umbrella of occupants of white-colour jobs.

Another notable point is that we, the Indians, refuse to learn or fail to learn from our past experiences, especially from the freedom movement. Here I like to mention the names of two persons who are globally respected because of their lifelong devotion to the cause of human values and human rights—Mahatma Gandhi and Nelson Mandela. It is interesting to know that the citizens of the developing countries, especially India, have failed to learn from the freedom struggle launched under the moral leadership of Mahatma Gandhi and several eminent persons who fought for independence of the country. Mahatma Gandhi is well known and well respected by the world even today because of his lifelong devotion to the cause of the democratic way of life or democracy. He used mainly two weapons—*Satyagraha* and *Ahimsa*—throughout the freedom struggle and practiced them till the end of his life. He had strong belief that these were two basic weapons which could save democracy. Unfortunately, the Indians have yet to learn from the freedom struggle, especially the significance of human values in the democracy.

We have also forgotten the lifelong sacrifice made by another world leader, Nelson Mandela, who died only on 5th December, 2013, whose "speech from Dock" made him immortal. On 9th October, 1963 Mandela joined ten others on trial for sabotage what became known as the "Rivonia Trial". While facing the death penalty Mandela said from the Dock, "I have fought against white domination and I have fought against black domination. I have cherished the ideal of a democratic and free society in which all persons live together in harmony and with equal opportunities. It is an ideal which I hope to love for and to achieve. But if needs be, it is an ideal for which I am prepared to die." He never wavered in his devotion to democracy, equality and learning. Despite terrible provocation he never answered racism with racism. His life is an inspiration to all who are oppressed and deprived and to all who oppose oppression and deprivation.[1]

We must start war against endemic corruption penetrated into every walk of life of the people. It is needed for the survival of the nation with human dignity. The moral dimension of Indian democracy is rooted in our culture and customs and traditions. What is needed today is to put a stop to the fast erosion of our human culture that originated in the ancient traditional society, though in a rudimentary form. The erosion of human culture provides scope for activism of irrational elements of the individuals under the control of money power as well as muscle power by dehumanizing the human society. The negative impact of it is felt in every walk of our life. Unfortunately, corruption has become a global phenomenon. United Nations Organization also taking steps for prevention of corruption in different nations of the world.

Today India is talking about good governance at a time when corruption is at the climax destroying the basic foundation of democracy. The people have lost trust in the government. Almost all public organizations are demoralized. Economic distortion in the public sector provides the scope to feel that the citizens of the country who are also the tax payers are exploited to the fullest extent. The modern Indian political leadership is still thinking that the concept of democracy confines to the election system only. The system of election is also reduced to the level of emotional game which can easily be played with the help of cash-for-vote and false promises. The voters are prevented to cast the vote by exercising their reasoning capacity.

The cornerstone of our democracy is fresh elections at least once in five years but the elective process has been infected by the purchasing power of the plutocracy. Elections are losing their common credibility and democratic value.[2]

Now time has come to re-humanize the Indian society. For

this there is an urgent need of a non-violent war against corruption to clear the path of flourishing human values and dignity. In this non-violent war every Indian must work as a warrior. This war is nothing but a war of establishment of good governance or democratic governance with due care to moral and ethical dimension.

Concept, Nature and Scope

The modern concept of Sovereign State and Citizenship invite the legal system of Rule of Law. The state has developed the system of salary to be paid to its officials and employees for rendering service to the state which is based on certain universally accepted principles like, equal pay for equal work, technique or qualifications required for job, market value, fundamental requirements of a man etc. Simultaneously, the citizens are also considered as taxpayers who pay tax for enjoying the services received from the state. But in course of time corruption penetrates into the civil service causing damage to the whole concept of democratic administration in the modern sovereign state. The wider concept of corruption highlights the behaviour of an occupant of a position which deviates from the formal duties of a public servant in the private interest. In the narrower sense it indicates the confinement to pecuniary benefits or bribe. While referring to corruption in wider sense it covers a whole host of vices attributable to the misuse of public office or authority for private ends. In this sense corruption includes all forms of dishonest gains in cash, kind or position by public servants.

The Indian Penal Code define as—

> "Whoever being or expecting to be a public servant, accepts or obtains, or agrees to accept, or attempts to obtain from any person for himself or for any other person, any gratification whatever, other than legal remuneration, as a motive or reward for doing or forebearing to do any official act or for showing or forebearing to show, in the exercise of his official functions, favour or disfavour to any person, or rendering or attempting to render any service or disservice to any person, with the Central or any State Government or Parliament or the Legislature of any State or with any local authority, Corporation or

Government Company referred to in Section 21, or with any public servant, as such shall be punished with imprisonment, the term of which may be extended up to three years or with fine, or both."

Corruption is an act of a person with concealed ill-motive. A corrupt person involves in unethical, illegal and inhuman activities to satisfy his or her greed. It is a demoralized state of administration in a country or in any organization. It may also be defined as an act of dishonesty of a person to acquire personal gain at the cost of public interest. Since Independence the Government of India is making efforts to eradicate corruption through conceptualization of the problem and formulation of various laws and regulations, in addition to the constitutional provisions. Immediately after Independence the Prevention of Corruption Act, 1947 was passed. It includes within the scope of corruption following types of misbehaviour:

- If a public servant is habitually accepts or obtains or agrees to accept or attempts to obtain from any person for himself or for any other person, any gratification as a motive or reward (other than remuneration) as a motive or reward such as is mentioned in the Indian Penal Code;
- If a public servant accepts or obtains or agrees to accept or attempts to obtain for himself or for any other person, any valuable thing without consideration or for a consideration which he knows to be inadequate, from any person whom he knows to have been, or to be, or to be likely to be concerned in any proceeding or business transacted or about to be transacted by him, or having any connection with the official functions of himself or of any public servant to whom he is subordinate, or from any person whom he knows to be interested in or related to the person so concerned; or
- If a public servant dishonestly or fraudulently misappropriates or otherwise converts for his own use any property entrusted to him or under his control as a public servant or allows any other person so to do;
- If he, by a corrupt or illegal means or by otherwise abusing his position as public servant, obtains for himself or for any other person any valuable or pecuniary advantage; or

- If he, or any person on his behalf is in possession, for which the public servant cannot satisfactorily account, or for pecuniary resources or property disproportionate to his known sources of income;
- Any public servant who commits criminal misconduct shall be punishable with imprisonment for a term which shall not be less than one year but which may be extended to seven years and shall also be liable to fine:
  Provided that the court may, for any special reasons recorded in writing, impose a sentence of imprisonment of less than one year."

The Representation of the People Act, 1950 includes within its definition political malpractices also as below:

(i) Bribery.
(ii) Undue influence.
(iii) Appeals to vote or refrain from voting on the grounds of religion, race, caste, community or language or the use of, or appeal to religious or national symbols.
(iv) Promotion or attempt to promote enmity between classes.
(v) Publication of false statements as to personal character or conduct or candidature of candidates.
(vi) Hiring or procuring of vehicles for the conveyanace of electors to or from polling stations.
(vii) Incurring or authorising of expenditure in contravention of Section 77 of the Representation of the People Act.
(viii) Obtaining or procuring assistance of persons in Government service."[3]

The definition given by the Santhanam Committee on Corruption indicates nature and scope of corruption. The definition is as below:

> "The problem of corruption is complex having roots and ramifications in society as a whole. In its widest connotation corruption includes improper or selfish exercise of power and influence attached to a public office or to the special position one occupies in public life. In this sense, the problem would have to be viewed in relation

to the entire system of moral values and socio-economic structure of society."[4]

In 1988 the Prevention of Corruption Act was passed by the Parliament of India to combat corruption in government agencies and public sector business in India. Following are the crimes punishable by law under this Act:

- "When a public servant accepts money or gifts over and above their salary, in return for favouring a person in their official duty.
- When a public servant accepts gifts from a person with whom they have a business or official relationship without paying them.
- When a public servant is guilty of criminal misconduct such as regularly accepting bribes to favour people during their official duty.
- If any person accepts money or gifts in return for influencing the public servant by using his personal connection or through illegal or corrupt methods, this person can also be punished.
- Any person helping the public servant commit these crimes can also be punished.
- According to the recent amendment in the act of a person offering the gift or a bribe will also be punished."[5]

This Act of 1988 added a new provision to the Act states that an act of a person offering the gift or a bribe will also be punished. (Prevention of Corruption Act, 1988). It may also be defined as misuse of power for both monetary as well as non-monetary gain for himself or herself.

David H. Bayley says, corruption is a general term covering misuse of authority as a result of consideration of personal gain, which may not be monetary. J.S. Nye defines corruption as behaviour which deviates from the formal duties of a public role because of private gain. This private role may be in the context of his own, close family, private clique. M.P. Sharma has simplified the definition with the help of certain common instances—violation of formal duties includes bribery (use of compensation to pervert the judgment of a person in a position of trust); nepotism (bestowal of patronage positions by reason of ascriptive relationships rather than merit); misappropriation (illegal allocation of public resources for private use; wilful failure to enforce laws or invoke sanctions that are appropriate to a situation.[6]

While analyzing the concept of corruption in the face of the modern concept of integrity of public servants it is difficult to ignore certain significant issues, like ethical framework for performance of duty, safeguard of human rights and human dignity, rule of law and interaction between civil service and society. The Santhanam Committee in it is report has stated that the modern concept of integrity of public servants in the sense that they should not use their official position to obtain any kind of financial or other advantage for themselves, their families or friends. Levy of taxes by law, parliamentary control over expenditure, regulation of conduct of public servants by rules, the breach of which is punishable also contributed to the concept of integrity of public servants.[7]

Major Factors Responsible for Corruption: The most important factors responsible for corruption are—

- The nature of human being. The people in general, have weakness for luxuries and comforts as a result of which they get themselves involved in all kinds of unethical activities.
- Moral and spiritual values are not given utmost importance in education system.
- Punishments imposed on the criminals are inadequate.
- Lifestyle of political leaders and political culture.
- People of India fail to acquire power from education.[8]

The discussions about causes of corruption as indicated by Alexandra Mills show that environment, attitude, administrative process contribute to a large extent the emergence of corrupt practices in the public administration. The social, political, organizational environments constitute a major cause of corruption. While talking about attitude it may be said that attitude of the employee is conditioned by the values adhered by the society and family members and colleagues in the organization. Next is the administrative system and the process. Increased competition and commercialization of an agency may lead to more opportunities to obtain personal benefits. The pressure of competition and administrative uncertainty may also widen the scope for corruption. Somehow the belief is created in the mind of the perpetrator that corruption will not be detected. Even if it is detected the perpetrator will be able to escape from punishment.

A study based on perpetrator interviews produced nine propositions about the process of "becoming corrupt" (Graaf and Huberts, 2008):

- Next to material gain the most important motives for officials to become corrupt are friendship or love and status and making an impression on colleagues and friends.
- Officials "slide down" towards corruption; most processes of becoming can be considered a slippery slope.
- Often corrupt officials have dominant and strong personalities, know how to "get things done", take or get the freedom to do things independently, and overstep formal boundaries of authority.
- More "business type" public officials bring the risk of more corruption.
- In most corruption cases, supervision of the corrupt officials is not strong.
- In most corruption cases, management has not promoted a clear integrity policy.
- Because of loyalty and solidarity, colleagues are hesitant to report suspicions of another's corrupt activities.
- The relationship between briber and the official is most enduring.

Corrupt officials including those who operate outside so-called corrupt networks, do not limit their corruption to one incident.[9]

The corruption occurs in a mind of a person when he has a motivation and an opportunity to act corruptly. Generally, when the person considers the scope of detection or punishment is low he or she is motivated to be involved in corrupt practices. On several occasions low salary or low income or poverty also provides scope to be involved in corruption. Unfortunately, it is noticed that high income group people or highly paid officials are more corrupt than the lower income group or poor people. Interestingly, they also exploit the ignorance or illiteracy of the ignorant masses to strengthen their hands in the field of corruption. Most of such ignorant people do not know that some of the activities performed by them at the instance of high officials or moneyed people are crimes. They have certain weak points—poverty, ignorance and respect for high officials and moneyed people. These weak points are knocked by the opportunists to satisfy the greed of the corrupt people.

When searching for the reasons of being corrupt after receiving heavy amount of money in the form of salary various factors are coming to light—heavy pressure from the family for luxurious life, competition amongst relatives or colleagues or neighbours in acquiring modern paraphernalia, availability of new products of companies at the door steps and pushing methods adopted by them, lack of understanding or confusion on the concept of "Standard of human living", inability to make distinction between greed and human need, confusion in ethical framework of social life, polluted socio-political environment in which human qualities in man disappear allowing activism of greed, emotions etc. whereby distortion of social values has begun leading to inactiveness of thinking capability man as human being, restless running after money without knowing where to stop etc.

The transactions with business men like contractors, suppliers, big companies increase the temptation to be corrupted in the case of office personnel from top to bottom. These business people are generally expert in motivating them through indirect way and in many cases they are successful in convincing the honest people that a particular act or behaviour is not a corrupt act or behaviour. The provision for high level technology and complicated red-tapism in public administration widens the scope for corruption in the process of delivering service to the people. Thus in most cases the meeting points of the government agencies and private actors are the fertile soil for emergence of corrupt practices.[10]

The scope for corruption is wide in a state with multifarious functions which require professional expert to carry out those functions. Enough scope for it is also found in a newly born states with developmental policies. In a modern democratic state which depends heavily on large contingent of public servants, and which is exposed to new or changing global environment due to progress of science and technology, growth of population, emphasis on welfare concept in administration and decentralization in administration, assertion on individual as well as group rights etc. widens the scope of corruption in administration.

When India became independent the country faced numerous problems originated due to World War Second, Freedom Struggle and departure of a large number of experienced high officials. Among them were, lack of industry, dependence of agricultural activities on traditional system, low income, unemployment and underemployment problems. Educational as well as social backwardness in rural areas, lack of exposure to outside world of the rural masses, very poor communication system, lack of enough health care facilities etc. the newly elected Governments gave priorities to the economic development of the country. Major reforms and reconstruction activities were directed towards this end. The process of modernization of the society started without delay since independence. Care was not taken to examine the social values of traditional society. It is true that various social values required today, i.e. in the modern democratic society were flourished during freedom movement launched under the leadership of Mahatma Gandhi, but modern independent India failed to grasp the power of those values. Experience shows that old system of values was discarded mercilessly.

Though the Indian economy occupies one of the top positions in the world, its growth has been uneven across social and economic groups. The uneven distribution of wealth is the product of endemic corruption in the country. The cost of corruption, perceptible in public sector inefficiencies and inadequate infrastructure, is undermining efforts to reduce poverty and promote sustainable growth.

Most reports and studies emphasize that the country continues to face major governance challenges. There is a lack of transparency in governance rules, procedures are complicated and the bureaucracy enjoys broad discretionary power. Nepotism is embedded in the civil service. Bureaucratic corruption pervades the Indian administrative system with widespread practices of bribery, nepotism and political corruption.[11]

The Santhanam Committee has rightly said, "the fixity of ways and aspirations of former times and the and operation of moral code tending towards austerity, frugality and simplicity of life, profoundly influenced the mechanism of social control and social responses. In the emerging Indian society with its emphasis on purposively initiated process of urbanization, alongside of the weakening of the social mores of the simpler society, signs are visible of materialism, growing impersonalism, importance of status resulting from the possession of money and economic power, group loyalties, intensification of parochial affinities, unwillingness or inability to deal with deviations from the highest standards of political, economic and social ethics, profession of faith in the rule of law and disregard thereof where adherence thereto is not convenient."

In independent India the new responsibilities of government resulted multiplication of the administrative processes. In this context the Law Commission pointed out in its fourteenth report that there is a vast field of administrative activities which the administrative authority could work outside the jurisdiction of law. It resulted difficulties in the redress of public grievances administrative power including discretionary power was vested to all levels of administrative hierarchy. The members at all levels were not endowed with same level of understanding capacity and strength of character. Where there is power and discretion, there is always possibility of abuse. It is more so when these powers have to be exercised in the face of scarcity and controls and pressure of spending public money.

The Santhanam Committee further pointed out that it was of the opinion that two major contributory factors were—first the partially acknowledged unwillingness to deal drastically with corrupt and inefficient public servants and, secondly, the protection given to the services in India, which is greater than that available in the more advanced countries. Some of the heads of departments confessed that, even where they were morally convinced that one of the officials working under them was corrupt, they were unable to do anything because of the difficulties in obtaining formal proof. They could not even make an adverse entry in the confidential roll without their being required to justify such an entry with proof when it was challenged after its communication to the government servant concerned. Article 311 of the Constitution as interpreted by our courts has made it very difficult to deal with corrupt public servants. When the question of amendment of the article came up before parliament the question of corruption was altogether ignored and overwhelming stress was laid upon protection of the individual government servant. This is an important issue which deserves to be urgently reconsidered by parliament.

Strict adherence to a high standard of ethical behaviour is necessary for honest functioning of new social, political and economic processes. The inability of all sections of the society to appreciate the need of it results in the emergence of the laws, this is dangerous because they cause irreparable damage to public morals.

The committee admitted that a large majority of officials incorruptible and are likely to react strongly against any direct attempt to subvert their integrity, the liaison and contact men make a careful study of the character, tastes and weaknesses of officials with whom they may have to deal and that weaknesses of officials are exploited. The contractors and suppliers are experts in the art of getting approved of the sub-standard works or to create favourable atmosphere to do so. Possession of large amount of unaccounted money by various classes is a major impediment in the purification of public life.[12]

Corruption in India: An Overview: Indian administration is constrained by corruption since ancient time. One can refer to *Arthasashtra*. Kautilya dealt with the problem of corruption in his book '*Arthasashtra*'. Kautilya identifies different types of embezzlement including bribery, graft, favouritism, frauds, manipulation of prices of commodities, inflation in salaries, theft in departments of the government etc. He pointed out the negative impact of corruption in administration, such as administrative inefficiency, obstruction to development of the nation etc. At the same time, he also realized the difficulties of removing corruption from administration. He suggested strengthening of monitoring system to locate corrupt officials, maintenance of strict discipline in administration and to make provision for punishment of corrupt officials.

Ashoka, the great Indian Emperor of the Maurya Dynasty, who embraced the teachings of Budhism suggested adoption of speedy administrative process to minimize corruption in administration.

During the Mughal period prevalence of '*bakshish*' as a reward to government employees even for routine tasks created a favourable environment for corruption in administration.

During East India Company corruption penetrated to each

and every field of administration. Almost all company personnel were involved in corrupt practices.[13]

Till the beginning of second, World War corruption was prevalent in considerable way amongst Revenue, Police, Excise and Public Works Departments. It was confined in the lower grade officials of these Departments and higher officials were almost free from this ailment. The limited number of functions of state, 'great depression' and lack of fluid resources limited the scope and capacity to corrupt or be corrupted. But immense war efforts during 1930 to 1945 which involved an annual expenditure of hundreds of cores over all kinds of war supplies and contracts created unprecedented opportunities for acquisition of wealth by doubtful means. The war time controls and scarcities provided ample opportunities for bribery, corruption, favouritism etc. The government subordinated all other considerations to that of making the war effort success.[14]

Even after gaining Independence and gaining power of self-rule, India could not be saved from corrupt or unethical behaviour of the administrators, political leaders, business men etc. However, at the initial stage of administration due to the leadership of several eminent persons in politics and administration corruption could not have its way in the country easily. Gradually emphasis on economic development and other developmental and welfare policies of the governments widens the path of corruption in administration. The autonomy of the experts, wide discretion of high officials, frequent contact of the officials and business leaders, appearance of middlemen in-between administrator and businessmen, political leaders and public etc. brought the situation from bad to worse. As a result corruption which was found in the war related departments like supply, public works, railways etc. travelled very comfortably to other public agencies. It increased and is still increasing in the country both in the political and administrative worlds in the main forms of funds embezzlement, bribery, fraudulent procurement practices etc. High ranking officials have also been involved in major corruption scandals.

The sectors most affected by corruption include public procurement, tax and customs administration, infrastructure, public utilities, and the police. The latter has been identified as one of the most corrupt institutions by various surveys. Today the educational, judicial institutions are also not free from this blame.

The media has widely published allegations of corrupt Indian citizens stashing millions of rupees in Swiss banks. Swiss authorities denied these allegations, which were later proven in 2015-16. It is alleged that the Indian media is largely controlled by extremely corrupt politicians and industrialists who play a major role by misleading the public with incorrect information and use the media for mud-slinging at political and business opponents.

Political Corruption: Corruption in India is a problem that has implications for protecting the *rule of law* and ensuring access to justice. As of December 2009, 120 of India's 524 Parliament Members were accused of various crimes, under India's First Information Report procedure wherein anyone can allege another to have committed a crime. Many of the biggest scandals since 2010 have involved high level government officials, including Cabinet Ministers and Chief Ministers, such as the 2010 Commonwealth Games Scam [Rs. 70,000 crore (US$ 11 billion)], the Adarsh Housing Society Scam, the Coal Mining Scam (Rs.1.86 lakh crore (US$ 28 billion), the Mining Scandal in Karnataka and Cash for Vote Scams.[15]

Corruption in politics of India has become open secret to the people. The voters both within and outside the Parliament and State Legislature face cash-for-vote system. Corrupt politicians are scot-free, unharmed and unpunished. People will not forget the alleged Commonwealth Game Corruption in 2010, Bofors payoff scandal of 1986 a total amount of Rs.1750 crore in purchase of guns from a Swedish firm for the army, the cement scandal of 1982 in Maharashtra, Sugar scam of 1994 involved a Union Minister of State for Food, Hawala scandal of 1991, the coffin-gate, fodder scam, even today allegations of corruption against Union Ministers are focused by media. However, India has political leaders like Lal Bahadur Shastri, Sardar Vallabh Bhai Patel who had very little bank balance at the time of death.[16]

Even at the state level India had Chief Minister like Sarat Chandra Sinha of Assam who could cut his requirements to the barest minimum. He led a very simple life and walked out from the office of Chief Minister to his residence with a bag in his hand after completion the term of office. Similar example may be referred in the case of the Chief Minister of Tripura, Manik Chandra Sarkar who led the life like a common man while in the office of Chief Minister.

Bureaucratic Corruption: Allegations are found in this context which say both government regulations and police share in bribe money, to the tune of 43 per cent and 45 per cent each, respectively. The *en route* stoppages at checkpoints and entry-points can take up to 11 hours per day. About 60 per cent of these (forced) stoppages on roads by concerned authorities, such as government regulators, police, forest, sales and excise, octroi, and weighing and measuring departments, are for extorting money. The loss in productivity due to these stoppages is an important concern; the number of truck trips could increase by 40 per cent, if forced delays are avoided. According to a 2007 World Bank published report, the travel time for a Delhi-Mumbai trip could be reduced by about 2 days per trip if corruption and associated regulatory stoppages to extract bribes were eliminated.

A 2009 survey of the leading economies of Asia revealed Indian bureaucracy to be not only the least efficient out of Singapore, Hong Kong, Thailand, South Korea, Japan, Malaysia, Taiwan, Vietnam, China, Philippines and Indonesia, but that working with India's civil servants was a "slow and painful" process.

Land and Property: In case of several Officials allegations are that they steal state property. In cities and villages throughout India, groups of municipal and other government officials, elected politicians, judicial officers, estate developers and law enforcement officials acquire, develop and sell land in illegal ways. Such officials and politicians are very well protected by the immense power and influence they possess.

Hospitals and Health Care: In government hospitals, it is alleged that corruption is associated with non-availability/ duplication of medicines, obtaining admission, consultations with doctors and receiving diagnostic services.

National Rural Health Mission is another healthcare-related government programme that has been subject to large scale corruption allegations. This social spending and entitlement programme hoped to improve health care delivery across rural India. Managed since 2005 by the Ministry of Health, the Indian government mandated a spending of Rs. 2.77 lakh crore (US$ 42 billion) in 2004-05, and increased it annually to be about 1 per cent India's gross domestic product. The National Rural Health Mission programme has been clouded by a large corruption scandal in which high-level government appointed officials were arrested, several of whom died under mysterious circumstances including one in prison. Corruption, waste and fraud-related losses from this government programme has been alleged to be Rs.1 lakh core (US $ 15 billion).

Income Tax Department: The allegation against this department is that there have been several cases of collusion involving officials of the Income Tax Department of India for preferential tax treatment and relaxed prosecutions in exchange for bribes.

Driver licensing: It is alleged on the basis of a study conducted between 2004 and 2005 found that India's driver licensing procedure was hugely distorted bureaucratic process and allows drivers to be licensed despite their low driving ability through promoting the usage of agents. Individuals with the willingness to pay make a significant payment above the official fee and most of these extra payments are made to agents, who act as an intermediary between bureaucrats and applicants.

The average licensee paid Rs. 1,080, approximately 2.5 times the official fee of Rs. 450, in order to obtain a licence. On average those who hired agents had a lower driving ability, with agents helping unqualified drivers obtain licences and bypass the legally required driving examination. Among the surveyed individuals, approximately 60 per cent of the license holders did not even take the licensing examination and 54 per cent of those licence holders failed an independent driving test.

Agents are the channels of corruption in this bureaucratic driver licensing system, facilitating access to licences among those who are unqualified to drive. Some of the failures of this system are caused by corrupt bureaucrats who collaborate with agents to drive by creating additional barriers within the system against those who did not hire agent.[17]

The licensing power is a regulatory power of the administrators over private individuals' activities. Professor L.D. White defines licence as "an official permit to carry on a particular business or profession or to do a particular thing otherwise forbidden." The licence is granted in conformity with certain standards or possession of certain qualifications laid down in advance.

The conditions or standards of regulation attached to licensing are—

- Skill or knowledge tested and certified by recognized examinations as in case of professional licences for the practice of medicine or law;
- Character and financial standing of the licence as in case of fire-arms licences in India or pawn shop licences in the Western countries;
- Consent or approval of the locality as in liquor licences;
- Public safety, for example in licences for storing inflammable materials and explosives; and
- Public health as in case of licensing of vendors or certain articles of food and drink; and
- Public utility and convenience as in case of licences to set up new public utilities or extend the existing one.

The main objectives of licensing are several—one objective is already mentioned above, i.e. preventive regulation of particular industries or activities with a view to prevent abuses and mal-practices detrimental to public safety, health and convenience. It may also be a means to an end. On many occasions licensing may be used as convenient method of raising and collecting revenue as in case of licensing of animals and vehicles by local bodies. It may also be a means of obtaining information and statistics about certain trades and occupations. It may be resorted to discourage and penalize certain undesirable trades or activities, for example, sale of liquor, lotteries, cross word puzzles etc.[18]

Professor Bibek Debroy and Laveesh Bhandari claim in their book *Corruption in India: The DNA and RNA* that public officials in India may be cornering as much as Rs. 921 billion (US$14 billion), or 1.26 per cent of the GDP through corruption. The book claims most bribery is in government delivered services and the transport and *real estate* industries. Bribery and corruption are pervasive, but some areas tend to more issues than others. A 2013 EY (Ernst & Young) Study reports the industries perceived to be the most venerable to corruption as: Infrastructure & Real Estate, Metals & Mining, Aerospace & Defence, and Power and Utilities. There are a range of specific factors that make a sector more susceptible to bribery and corruption risks than others. High use of middlemen, large value contracts, and liasioning activities etc. drive the depth, volume and frequency of corrupt practices in vulnerable sector.

A 2011 KPMG (Klynveld Peat Marwick Goerdeler) study

reports India's real estate, telecommunications and government-run social development projects as the three top sectors plagued by corruption. The study found India's defence, the information technology industry and energy sectors to be the most competitive and least corrupt prone sectors.

CMS (Content Management System) India in its 2010 India Corruption Study Report said that socio-economically weaker sections of Indian society are the most adversely affected by government corruption. These include the rural and urban poor, although the study claims that nationwide perception of corruption had decreased between 2005 and 2010. Over the 5-year period, a significantly greater number of people surveyed from middle and poorest classes in all parts of India claimed government corruption had dropped overtime, and that they had fewer direct experiences with bribery demands. Whereas in reality corruption has increased ten folds since 2010 and continues to grow relentlessly on a daily basis.

The table below compares the perceived anti-corruption effort across some major states in India. A rising index implies higher anti-corruption effort and falling corruption. According to this table, the states of Bihar and Gujarat have experienced significant improvements in their anti-corruption efforts, while conditions have worsened in the states of Assam and West Bengal. Consistent with the results in this table, in 2012 a BBC News report claimed the state of Bihar has transformed in recent years to become the least corrupt state in India.

Index Trends in Major States by Respective Anti-corruption Effort

State	*1990-95*	*1996-00*	*2001-05*	*2006-10*
Bihar	0.41	0.30	0.43	0.88
Gujarat	0.48	0.57	0.64	0.69
Andhra Pradesh	0.53	0.73	0.55	0.61
Punjab	0.32	0.46	0.46	0.60
Jammu & Kashmir	0.13	0.32	0.17	0.40
Haryana	0.33	0.60	0.31	0.37
Himachal Pradesh	0.26	0.14	0.23	0.35
Tamil Nadu	0.19	0.20	0.24	0.29
Madhya Pradesh	0.23	0.22	0.31	0.29
Karnataka	0.24	0.19	0.20	0.29

(Contd.)

State	*1990-95*	*1996-00*	*2001-05*	*2006-10*
Rajasthan	0.27	0.23	0.26	0.27
Kerala	0.16	0.20	0.22	0.27
Maharashtra	0.45	0.29	0.27	0.26
Uttar Pradesh	0.11	0.11	0.16	0.21
Odisha	0.22	0.16	0.15	0.19
Assam	0.21	0.02	0.14	0.17
West Bengal	0.11	0.08	0.03	0.01

Coming to the question of black money it refers to money that is not fully or legitimately the property of the 'owner'. A government white paper on black money in India suggests two possible sources of black money: the activities not permitted by the law, such as crime, drug trade, terrorism and corruption, all of which are illegal in India and secondly, wealth that may have been generated through lawful activity but accompanied by failure to declare income and pay taxes. Some of this black money ends up in illicit financial flows across international borders, such as deposits in tax haven countries.

Indian Black Money in Switzerland: India was ranked 38th by money held by its citizens in Swiss banks in 2004 but then improved its ranking by slipping to 61st position in 2015 and further improved its position by slipping to 75th position in 2016.

Domestic Black Money: Indian companies are reportedly misusing public trust for money laundering. India has no centralized repository- like the registrar of companies for corporate – of information on public trusts.

2016 Evasion Attempts After Note Ban

Gold purchases: In Gujarat, Delhi and many other major cities, sales of gold increased on 9th November, with an increased 20 per cent to 30 per cent premium surging price as much as Rs. 45,000 (US $ 690) from the ruling price of Rs. 31,900 (US $ 490) per 10 grams.

Donations: Authorities of Sri Jalakanteswarar temple at Vellore discovered cash worth of Rs. 4.4 million (US $ 67,000) from the temple Hundi.

Multiple bank transactions: There have also been reports of people circumventing the restrictions imposed on exchange transactions and attempting to convert black money into white by making multiple transactions at different bank branches. People were also getting rid of large amounts of banned currency by sending people in groups to exchange their money at banks. In response, the government announced that it would start marking customers with indelible ink.

This was in addition to other measures proposed to ensure that the exchange transactions are carried out only once by each person. On 17th November, the Government reduced the exchange amount to Rs. 2000 to discourage attempts to convert black money into legitimate money.

Railways booking: As soon as the demonetization was announced, it was observed by the Indian Railways authorities that a large number of people started booking tickets in classes 1A and 2A for the longest distances possible, to get rid of unaccounted for cash. A senior official said, "on November 13, 42.7 million passengers were nationally booked across all classes. Of these, only 1,209 were 1A and 16,999 for 2A. It is a sharp dip from the number of passengers booked on November 9, when 27,237 passengers had booked tickets in 1A and 69,950 in 2A.

The Railway Ministry and the Railway Board responded swiftly and decided that cancellation and refund of tickets of value Rs. 10,000 and above will not be allowed by any means involving cash. The payment can only be through cheque/electronic payment. Tickets above Rs. 10,000 can be refunded by filing ticket deposit receipt only on surrendering the original ticket. A copy of the PAN card must be submitted for any cash transaction above Rs. 50,000. The Railway Board claimed that since the Railway Board on 10th November imposed a number of restrictions to book and cancel tickets, the number of people booking 1A and 2A tickets came down.

Municipal and local tax payments: As the use of the demonetized notes had been allowed by the Government for payment of municipal and local body taxes, leading to people using the demonetized Rs. 500 and Rs. 1000 notes to pay large amounts of outstanding and advance taxes. As a result, revenue collections of the local civic bodies jumped. The Greater Hyderabad Municipal Corporation reported collecting about Rs. 1.6 billion

(US $ 25 million) in cash payments of outstanding and advance taxes within 4 days.

Axis Bank: Income Tax officials raided multiple branches of Axis Bank and found bank officials involved in acts of money laundering.

Business and Corruption: Public servants have very wide discretionary powers offering the opportunity to extort undue payments from companies and ordinary citizens. The awarding of public contracts is notoriously corrupt, especially at the state level. Scandals involving high-level politicians have highlighted the payment of kickbacks in the healthcare, IT and military sectors. The deterioration of the overall efficiency of the government, protection of property rights, ethics and corruption as well as undue influence on government and judicial decisions has resulted in a more business environment.

Judiciary: According to *Transparency International*, Judicial Corruption in India is attributable to factors such as "delays in the disposal of cases, shortage of judges and complex procedures, all of which are exacerbated by a preponderance of new laws". Over the years there have been numerous allegations against judges, and in 2011 a former judge at the Kolkata High Court became the first judge in India to be impeached by the Rajya Sabha for misappropriation of funds.[19]

REFERENCES

1. https://www.nelsonmandela.org/content/page/biography, dt.21/12/2018.
2. Iyer, V.R. Krishna (1980). *Justice and Beyond*, Deep and Deep Publications, New Delhi.
3. A.R. Tyagi (1989). *Public Administration*, 6th revised edition, Atma Ram & Sons, Delhi.
4. Santhanam Committee Report on Prevention of Corruption 1962.
5. https://en.wikipedia.org/wiki/Prevention_of_Corruption_Act_1988, dt. 3.10.2018
6. Sharma, Dr. M.P. and Dr. B.L. Sadana (2004). *Public Administration in Theory and Practice*; Kitab Mahal, Allahabad, 40th reprint.
7. https://www.civilservicein india.com/subject/corruption-in-india 1html dt 24.12.2018.
8. https://www.invstopedia.com/terms/o/oecd.asp dated 29.6.2018

9. unpan/un.org/intradoc/groups/public/documents/un-padm/ unpan049589-pdf 30.6.2018.
10. http://www.preservearticles.com/2012031427266/what-are-the-causes-of-administrative-corruption-in-india.html. Accessed on 27.6.2018.
11. cvc.nic.in/sites/default/files/ault/scr_rpt_cvc.pdf. accessed on 4.8.2018
13. Arora, K. Ramesh and Rajni Goyal (1996). *Indian Public Administration Institutions and Issues*; 2nd edition; Wishwa Prakashan, New Delhi.
14. cvc,nic.in/sites/default/files/ault/scr_rpt_cvc.pdf 4.8.2018.
15. https://en.wikipedia.org/wikiCorruption_in_India. Accessed on 24.5.2018.
16. https://www.civilserviceindia.com/subject/essay/corruption-in-india.html, accessed on 18.6.2018.
17. https://en.wikipedia.org/wikiCorruption_in_India. Accessed on 24.5.2018.
18. Sharma, M.P. and Dr. B.L. Sadana; (2004); *Public Administration in Theory and Practice*: Kitab Mahal, New Delhi.
19. https://en.wikipedia.org/wiki/corruption_in_India dt 25/12/218.

II

Preventive Measures

International and National Levels

As regards anti-corruption efforts at the international level mention may be made of two Conventions – OECD Anti Bribery Convention and the United Nations Convention Against Corruption.

The World Bank Group, under the leadership of James David Wolfensohn as its ninth President (1995–2005) has done a pioneering service to reduce corruption at the global level. Under the leadership of Wolfensohn the World Bank implemented a range of significant reforms to help achieve its mission and broke new ground in several major areas, including corruption, debt, relief, disability, the environment and gender.

At his first annual meeting of World Bank Group in 1995 Wolfensohn announced that a major theme of his presidency would be to forge "a new compact between donors, investors, and recipients to ensure that resources are sufficient to meet the needs of the world's poorest people—and that those resources are used efficiently and transparently." In the next annual meeting of the Group held in 1996. Wolfensohn told in the meeting that the Bank needed to "work on the second part of the compact to ensure that all resources are used efficiently." He also informed the delegates in one of his speeches that "if the new compact is to succeed, we must tackle the issue of economic and financial efficiency. But we also need to address transparency, accountability, and institutional capacity. Let us not to mince words: we need to deal with the Bank's assistance to Governments who would implement national programmes to discourage corrupt practices. Wolfensohn set up an Internal Task Force, the Corruption Action Plan Working Group, to develop a systematic framework for addressing corruption as a developmental issue. The Group's report "Helping Countries to Combat Corruption: the Role of World Bank" appeared in the annual meeting in 1997. It argued that Bank needed "to place a concern for corruption in the mainstream of its operational work and research" and as part of that to "raise the impact of corruption in its dialogue with Borrowers." And "to address corruption and reduce international bribery." And pointed out to the OECD-led initiatives to combat bribery in international business transactions. Corruption is no longer a taboo subject in the Bank, it declared.[1]

The full form of OECD is Organization for Economic Cooperation and Development. It is a group of 34 member countries that discuss and economic and social policy. OECD was established on 14th December, 1960 by 18 European nations plus US and Canada. It has expanded over time to include members from South America and Asia Pacific region. It includes most of the highly developed countries.

The OECD is variously referred to as a think tank or monitoring group. It stated goals include fostering economic development and cooperation, fighting poverty and ensuring the environmental impact of growth and social development.

While looking to its background in finds that in 1948, in aftermath of Second World War the Organization for European Economic Cooperation (OEEC) was established to administer the predominating US funded Marshal Plan for post-War reconstruction on the continent. The group emphasized the importance of working together for economic development with the goal of avoiding more dealers of European warfare. The OEEC was instrumental in helping the European Economic Community which has since evolved into the European Union to established a European Free Trade Area.[2]

In 1989 the OECD established an *ad hoc* working group for comparative review of national legislations regarding the bribery of foreign public officials. In 1994 the OECD Ministerial Council adopted the recommendation of the "Council on Bribery in International Business Transactions". The Convention was signed on 17th December, 1997 and came into force on 15th February, 1999.

By acknowledging the ubiquity of corruption, the lasting damage it can cause and the responsibility of powerful institutions to take action, the speech caused a turning point in the attitude of the international actors and licensed a systematic international effort against corruption. Since then corruption has been studied, classified, measured, defined and prescribed by policy makers and practitioners, theorists and researchers mostly in the disciplines of political science, economics, philosophy, public administration and law.

The OECD aimed at reducing political corruption and corporate crime in developing countries by encouraging sanctions against bribery in International business transactions carried out by companies based in the convention member countries.

The countries that have signed the convention are required to put in place legislation that criminalizes the act of bribing a foreign public official. The OECD has no authority to implement the convention, but instead monitors implementation by participating countries *via* its Working Group on Bribery. Countries are responsible for implementing laws and regulations that conform to the Convention and, therefore, provide for enforcement.[3]

In 2009 some significant recommendations of the convention were released on 9th December, 2009 when OECD marked the tenth anniversary celebration of the entry into force of the OECD Convention on Combating Bribery of Foreign Public Officials in International Business Transactions (OECD Anti-Bribery Convention).

All the state parties to the OECD are called to—

- Adopt best practices for making companies liable for foreign bribery so that they cannot be misused as vehicles for bribing foreign public officials and they cannot avoid detection, investigation and prosecution for such bribery by using agents and intermediaries, including foreign subsidies, to bribe for them;
- Periodically review polices and approach on small facilitation payments. These are legal in some countries if the payment is made to a government employee to speed up an administrative process;

- Improve cooperation between countries for the sharing of information and evidence in foreign bribery investigations and prosecutions and the seizure, confiscation and recovery of the proceeds of transnational bribery, through, for instance, improved or new agreements between the states parties for these purposes;
- Provide effective channels for public officials to report suspected foreign bribery internally within the public service and externally to the law enforcement authorities, and for protecting whistleblowers from retaliation; and
- Working with private sector to adopt more stringent internal controls, ethics and compliance programmes and measures to prevent and detect bribery.

The 36 OECD countries and 8 non-OECD countries—Argentina, Brazil, Bulgaria, Colombia, Costa Rica, Peru, Russia and South Africa signed the Convention. As regards implementation and enforcement of the recommendation the Convention itself establishes a peer-driven monitoring mechanism to ensure the thorough implementation of the international obligations that countries have taken on under the Convention. This monitoring is carried out by the OECD Working group on Bribery. The Working Group is made up of representatives from the state parties to the Convention and meets regularly.[4]

In addition to OECD there were several multilateral instruments to prevent and combat corruption, such as Inter-American Convention against Corruption adopted by the Organization of American States on 29th March, 1996, the Convention on the Fight against Corruption involving Officials of Member States of the European Union, adopted by the Council of the European Union on 26th May, 1997, the Convention on Corruption, adopted by the Committee of Ministers of the Council of Europe on 27th January, 1999, the Civil Law Convention on Corruption, adopted by the Committee of Ministers of the Council of Europe on 4th November, 1999 and the African Union Convention on Prevention and Combating Corruption adopted by the Heads of States and Governments of the African Union on July 2003.

Another effort at the international level at the initiative of United Nations of Organization is the United Nations Convention against Corruption (UNCAC) which came into force in December 2005, is the ever-first binding global anti-corruption instrument. It obliges the states to prevent and criminalize different corrupt practices, promote international cooperation, cooperate for the recovery of stolen assets and enhance technical assistance and information exchange. The Convention addresses both public and private spheres and provides a set of comprehensive agreed-upon obligations and provisions to criminalize corruption and enhance transparency and accountability. In order to monitor the progress in the implementation of the Convention, member-states have agreed to conduct "peer-review mechanisms" among themselves, for which UNODC acts as a Secretariat.

Kofi A. Annan, Secretary General of UN in his foreword to the Report of the United Nations Convention against Corruption said, "Corruption is an insidious plague that has wide range of corrosive effects on societies. It undetermined democracy and the rule of law, leads to violation of human rights, distorts markets, erodes the quality of life and allows organized crime, terrorism and other threats to human security to flourish.

This evil phenomenon is found in all countries—big or small, rich and poor—but it is in the developing world that its effects are most destructive. Corruption hurts the poor disproportionately by diverting funds intended for development, undermining a Government's ability to provide basic services, feeding inequality and injustice and discouraging foreign aid and investment. Corruption is a key element in economic underperformance and a major obstacle to poverty alleviation and development.

I am, therefore, very happy that we now have a new instrument to address this scourge at the global level. The adoption of the United Nations Convention against Corruption will send a clear message that the international community is determined to prevent and control corruption. It will warn the corrupt that betrayal of the public trust will no longer be tolerated. And it will reaffirm the importance of core values such as honesty, respect for the rule of law, accountability and transparency in promoting development and making the world a better place for all.

Kofi A. Annan pointed out in his foreword to resolution of UN that for the United Nations, the Convention is the culmination of work that started many years ago, when the word corruption was hardly ever uttered in official circles. It took systematic efforts, first at the technical, and then gradually at the political level to put the fight against corruption on the global agenda. Both the Monterrey International Conference on Financing for Development and Johannesburg World Summit on Sustainable Development offered opportunities for governments to express their determination to attack corruption and to make many people aware of the devastating effect that corruption has on development."[5]

The UN General Assembly, by a resolution on 4th December, 2000 established an *ad hoc* Committee for the negotiation of an effective international legal instrument against corruption and requested the Secretary General to convene an inter-governmental open-ended expert group to examine and prepare draft terms of reference for the negotiation of such instrument. Accordingly he convened a meeting of the inter-governmental expert group on 20th December, 2000 to examine the question of illegally transferred funds and the return of such funds to the countries of origin. The *Adhoc* Committee carried out its work at the headquarters of the United Nations Office on Drugs and Crime in Vienna, in which the Committee submitted its final text of the draft of the United Nations Convention against Corruption to the General Assembly for its consideration and action. The report was opened for signature at the High-level Political signing conference to be held in Merida, Mexico, from 9-11 December, 2003.

The Preamble to the Convention stated that the Convention concerned:

(a) The seriousness of the problems and threats posed by corruption to the stability and security of societies, undermining the institutions and values of democracy, ethical values and justice and jeopardizing sustainable development and the rule of law;
(b) About the links between corruption and other forms of crime, in particular organized crime and economic crime, including money laundering; and
(c) About cases of corruption that involve vast quantities of assets, which may constitute a substantial proportion of the resources of states, and that threaten the political stability and sustainable development of those states.

The States parties to the convention also convinced that:

(a) Corruption is no longer a local matter but a transnational phenomenon that effects all societies and economies, making international cooperation to prevent and control it essential;
(b) A comprehensive and multidisciplinary approach is required to prevent and combat corruption;
(c) The availability of technical assistance can play an important role in enhancing the ability of states, including by strengthening capacity and by institution-building, to prevent and combat corruption effectively; and
(d) The illicit acquisition of personal wealth can be particularly damaging to democratic institutions, national economies and the rule of law.

The states parties determined to prevent, detect and deter in a more effective manner international transfers of illicitly acquired assets and to strengthen international operation in asset recovery. They have in mind that the prevention and eradication of corruption is a responsibility of all states and that they must cooperate with one another, with the support and involvement of individuals and groups outside the public sector, such as civil society, non-governmental organizations and community-based organizations, if their efforts in this area are to be effective. They realize that to foster a culture of rejection of corruption there is the need of the principles of proper management of public affairs and public property, fairness, responsibility and equality before the law and safeguard of integrity.

The purposes of the Convention are:

(a) To promote and strengthen measures to prevent and combat corruption more efficiently and effectively;
(b) To promote, facilitate and support international cooperation and technical assistance in the prevention and fight against corruption, including in asset recovery; and
(c) To promote integrity, accountability and proper management of public affairs and property.

The Convention makes it clear that states parties shall carry out their obligations under the Convention in a manner consistent with the principles of sovereign equality and territorial integrity of states and that of non-intervention in the domestic affairs of other states. No state party is entitled to undertake in the territory of another state the exercise of jurisdiction and performance of functions that are reserved exclusively for the authorities of that other state by its domestic law.

United Nations in its Convention against Corruption suggested several preventive measures to prevent corruption which may be adopted by the member states. These are:

1. **Anti-corruption Practices and Policies**: The state may formulate effective and coordinated anti-corruption policies reflecting the principles of rule of law, effective management of public affairs and public property, integrity, transparency and accountability. These policies must provide scope for public participation in the process. The state may make periodic evaluation of the legal and administrative measures aiming to maintain their adequacy to prevent and fight against corruption. Mutual collaboration amongst states and also with international and regional organizations is essential through participation in international programmes and projects on prevention of corruption.

2. **Establishment of Institutions**: The state may establish institutions as anti-corruption bodies to take effective preventive measures. The main functions of these bodies will be to oversee and coordinate policies, disseminate knowledge about preventive measures against corruption. These bodies must be independent and free from undue influence. However, the state must provide required man and material including training to the staff to carry out their functions.

3. **Public Sector**: Endeavour has to be made to strengthen systems of recruitment, hiring, retention, promotion and retirement of civil servants: (i) based on the principles of efficiency, transparency and objective criteria such as merit, equity and aptitude; (ii) adequate care has to be taken to train the personnel in the positions considered vulnerable to corruption; (iii) provisions should be made for adequate remuneration and equitable pay scales; (iv) promotion of education and training programmes to enable the officials to meet the requirements for the correct, honourable and proper performance of public functions and that provide them specialization in the field. Appropriate measures should be taken

to prescribe criteria concerning candidature for and election to public office and to maintain transparency in funding of candidature for election and to political parties.

4. Codes of Conduct of Public Officials: Provisions may be made of codes of conduct for maintaining honesty, integrity and responsibility of the public officials. The International Code of Conduct of Public Officials (UN General Assembly adopted the resolution in 1996) may also be consulted while preparing the code of conduct by a state. Public officials may be encouraged to report to the authority of corrupt practices whenever such acts come to their notice. Public officials may be encouraged to declare their outside activities, employment, investment, assets and substantial gifts or benefits from which a conflict of interest may result with regard to the functions as public officials. Provision should be made for punishing the public officials who violate the codes of conduct.

5. Public Procurement and Management of Public Finances: It is necessary to establish necessary systems of procurement, based on transparency, competition and objective criteria on decision-making, that are effective, in preventing corruption. For this purpose, certain steps have to be taken, such as:

(a) Sufficient time must be given as regards distribution of information relating to procurement procedures and contracts, including information on invitations to tender and relevant or pertinent information on the award of contracts to prepare and submit tenders;

(b) Conditions for participation must be declared much in advance, including selection and award criteria and tendering rules and their publication;

(c) The use of objective and predetermined criteria for public procurement decisions is essential to facilitate the subsequent verification of the correct application of the rules and procedures;

(d) Violation of the rules relating to procurement must be punishable and effective measures have to be taken for appeal; and

(e) Appropriate measures have to be taken to regulate matters regarding personnel responsible for procurement, such as declaration of interest in particular public procurement, screening procedures and training requirements.

Every state must adopt fundamental principles for promoting transparency and accountability in the management of public finances. Such measures will be:

(a) Procedures for the preparation of national budget;
(b) Timely reporting on revenue and expenditure;
(c) A system of accounting and auditing standards and related oversight;
(d) Efficient system of risk management; and
(e) Efficient system of correction in case of failure with the requirements of the principles.

Every state has to formulate principles to preserve integrity of accounting books, records, financial statements or other documents related to public expenditure and revenue and to prevent the falsification of such documents.

6. Public Reporting: Measures have to be taken to enhance transparency in its public administration, including with regard to organization, functioning and decision-making processes. Such measures may include:

(a) Adoption of procedures or regulations allowing members of the general public to obtain, where needed, information on the organization, functioning and decision-making process in the public administration, with due regard to the protection of privacy and personal data, on decisions and legal acts that concern members of the public;
(b) Simplifying administrative procedures to facilitate public to have access to the competent decision-making authorities; and
(c) Publishing information, which may include periodic reports on the risks of corruption in its public administration.

7. Measures relating to the Judiciary and Prosecution Services: Bearing in mind the independence of judiciary and its crucial role in combating corruption, each state may take measures to strengthen integrity and to prevent opportunities for the corruption among members of the judiciary. Such measures may include rules with respect to the conduct of members of the judiciary. It is applicable to those state parties which do not form part of judiciary.

8. Private Sector: Each state may take measures to prevent corruption in the private sector enhancing accounting and auditing standards. Measures to achieve these ends may include:

(a) Promotion of cooperation between law enforcement agencies and relevant private entities;
(b) Development of standards and procedures designed to safeguard the integrity of relevant private entities, including codes of conduct for the correct, honourable and proper performance of activities of business and all relevant professions and prevention of conflicts of interest. Attempt must be made to promote good commercial practices among businesses;
(c) Maintenance of transparency among private entities;
(d) Prevention of misuse of procedures regulating private entities; and
(e) Ensure of private enterprises, taking into account their structure and size, have sufficient internal auditing controls to assist in preventing and detecting acts of corruption and that accounts and required financial statements of such private enterprise are subject to appropriate auditing and certification procedures.

In order to prevent corruption, each state must take necessary measures for maintenance of books and records, financial disclosures and accounting and auditing standards to prohibit:

(i) Establishment of off-the-books accounts;
(ii) Making of off-the-books or inadequately identified transactions;
(ii) Recoding of non-existence;
(iv) Entry of liabilities with incorrect identification of their objects;
(v) Use of false documents;
(vi) Intentional destruction of book-keeping documents earlier than foreseen by law; and

(vii) There should be no tax deductibility of expenses that constitute bribes.

9. Participation of Society: State may take measures to promote public participation of individuals and groups outside the public sector, such as civil society, non-governmental organizations and community-based organizations, in the prevention of and the fight against corruption and to raise public awareness regarding the existence, causes and gravity of and threat posed by corruption. The participation may be strengthened by enhancing transparency of and promoting the contribution of public to the decision-making process:

(a) Undertaking public information activities that contribute to non-tolerance of corruption, as well as public education programmes, including school and university curricula;
(b) Ensuring that public has effective access to information;
(c) Respecting, promoting and protecting the freedom to seek, receive, publish and disseminate information concerning corruption. That freedom may be subject to certain restrictions, as are provided for law and are necessary:
  (i) For respect of the rights or reputation of others; and
  (ii) For protection of national security or ordure public or public health or morals.

10. Measures to prevent Money-laundering: Each state may institute a comprehensive regulatory and supervisory regime for banks and non-bank financial institutions, other bodies that are susceptible to money laundering, which regime shall emphasize requirements for customer and where appropriate, beneficial owner identification, record keeping and the reporting of suspicious transactions. Provision may also be made to establish a financial intelligence unit to serve as a national Centre for the collection, analysis and dissemination of information regarding potential money-laundering. The state may take feasible measures to detect and monitor the movement of cash and appropriate negotiable instruments across their borders, subject to safeguards to ensure proper use of information and without impeding in any way the movement of legitimate capital the state may consider implementing appropriate and feasible measures to require financial institutions, including money remitters:

(a) to include on forms for the electronic transfer of funds and related messages accurate and meaningful information on the obligation; and
(b) to maintain such information throughout the payment chain.

The state may also take measures to develop and promote global, regional, sub-regional and bilateral cooperation among judicial, law enforcement and financial regulatory authorities in order to combat money laundering (UN Convention against Corruption).

UNCAC is the only legally binding universal anti-Corruption instrument. The Convention's far-reaching approach and mandatory character of many of its provisions make its unique tool for developing a comprehensive response to a global problem. The Conference of the states parties is the main policy–making body of the Convention supporting state parties and signatories in their implementation of the convention into domestic law by states parties is through a unique peer-Review process evaluated.[6]

The United Nations Office of Drugs and Crime (UNODC) is a UN Office that was established in 1997 as the office for Drug Control and Crime Prevention by combining the UN International Drug Control Programme and the Crime Prevention and Criminal Justice Division in the UN Office at Vienna.

The UNODC operates in all regions of the world through an extensive network of field offices. UNODC relies on voluntary contributions, mainly from Governments, for 90 per cent of its budget.

UNODC is mandated to assist Member-States in their struggle against illicit drugs, crime and terrorism. In the Millennium Declaration, Member-States also resolved to intensify efforts to fight transnational crime in all its dimensions, to redouble the efforts to implement the commitment to counter the world drug problem and to take concerted action against international terrorism.

The pillars of the UNODC work programme are:

(i) Field-based technical cooperation projects to enhance the capacity of member States to counter illicit drugs, crime and terrorism;
(ii) Research and analytical work to increase knowledge and understanding of drugs and crime issues and expand the evidence base for policy and operational decisions; and
(iii) Normative work to assist States in the ratification and implementation of the relevant international treaties, the development of domestic legislation on drugs, crime and terrorism, and the provision of Secretariat and Substantive services to the treaty-based and governing bodies.

An overview of the technical assistance helps to understand that the international community confronts a host of menaces, including illicit drugs, threats to security and health and new and emerging crimes. As governments and other development partners increasingly look to UNODC for specialized assistance and expertise, the office has expanded its scope and volume of work to provide comprehensive and coherent responses to these challenges.

In October 2010 UNODC has released a new Menu of Services, which provides to know how clients can access targeted assistance or the range of publications and online tools available.

Following are the areas in which UNODC can help:[7]

Organized crime and trafficking: UNODC helps governments react to the instability and insecurity caused by crimes like smuggling of illicit drugs, weapons, natural resources, counterfeit goods and human beings between countries and continents. It is also addressing emerging forms of crime, such as cybercrime, trafficking in cultural arte facts and environmental crime.

Corruption: Corruption is a major impediment to economic and social development. UNODC partners with, the public and private sectors, as well as civil society, to loosen the grip that corrupt individuals have on government, national borders and trading channels. In recent years, the office has stepped up its efforts to help States recover assets stolen by corrupt officials.

Crime Prevention and Criminal Justice Reform: UNODC promotes the use of training manuals and the adoption of codes of conduct and standards and norms that aim to guarantee that the accused, the guilty and the victims can all rely on a criminal justice system that is fair and grounded on human rights value. A strong rule of law will also instill confidence among citizens in the effectiveness of the courts and the humanness of the prisons.

Drug Abuse Prevention and Health: Through educational campaigns and by basin its approach on scientific findings, UNODC tries to convince youth not to use illicit drugs, drug-dependent people to seek treatment and governments to see drug use as a health problem, not a crime.

Terrorism Prevention: On this issue UNODC is moving towards a more programmatic approach that involves developing long-term, customized assistance to entities involved in investigating and adjudicating cases linked to terrorism.

The nature of assistance may be expressed in the words of UNODC Executive Director Yuri Fedotovas, "If UNODC provides services that you require, or if you would like to support our work, please call on us. Working together to take action against drugs, crime, corruption and terrorism, we can increase security and improve the lives of individuals, families and communities all over the world."

https://www.unodc.org/unodc/en/about-unodc/index.html, dated 30.6.2018.

The Convention was adopted by the UN General Assembly on 31st October, 2003 at New York. India signed the Convention in 2005 and ratified it in 2011. It was due to the refusal of the UPA government, especially the Department of Personnel and Training. However, over the years MEA (Ministry of External Affairs, which is the nodal Ministry for international treaties) pushed the government to ratify it. The reason was the non-existence of domestic laws in the line of international convention. In the face of writings of scholars like Thompson, Rose-Ackerman, Pope, Anechiarico and Jacobs during 1990s the Convention also realized that total elimination of corruption is unrealistic; likely to be disproportionately costly, rigid and risk compromising human rights. The preferred goal of prevention is to achieve integrity of government so that it can perform its "intrinsic roles" efficiently and fairly (Thompson, 1992:255; Rose-Ackerman, 1996; Pope, 1999; Anechiarico and Jacobs, 1996).

The first step to adopt measures to curb corruption is to make diagnosis of the concept of corruption and to explore causes of it. It is a concept which has social, religious, moral, political, administrative and economic implications. The concept of corruption in its broader sense means misuse of entrusted power for private gain. Even if we consider the concept in broader perspective preventive measures require multi-faceted effort involving each and every individual and institution.

In a modern state corruption in public administration attracts attention of sections of the society. The term "public administration" means .... to be filled. Structurally it means agencies, authorities, departments, public offices, commissions etc. that deliver government policies and programmes financed by the government. Whitton stated that corruption may be referred as a failure of the institution of public service and as a betrayal of the essential professional ethics of the public administrator to serve the public "honestly and disinterestedly as trustees of the public interest" (Whitton, 1994:39). Theobald has very rightly said that historically the institutional culture of public administration has been a form of protection against corruption (Theobald, 1997) and supporting the professional integrity of public officials (UNODC, 2009).

The preventive provisions provided by UNCAC include more preventive and proactive measures such as enhancing transparency and public engagement, establishing standards, and reducing opportunities for corruption in high risks activities such as judiciary and public procurement. Significantly, these more preventive and proactive measures are left to States to implement according to local conditions but technical support is provided in the UNODC Technical Guide. It also suggested that while adopting preventive measures the study reports on both corruption and preventive techniques of International NGOs and academic research Centres can be used to develop skills and share best practice. Local efforts are also supported by regional capacity building programmes, such as those facilitated by the multilateral development banks, and initiatives that might be led by domestic integrity agencies such as public service commissions, anti-corruption agencies and aid donors.

The international commitment to achieve the Millennium Development Goals by 2015 added a note of urgency to the anti-corruption task since the major beneficiaries of those goals suffer due to corruption. The Millennium Development Goals were:

- Eradicate extreme poverty and hunger,
- Achieve universal primary education,

- Promote gender equality and empower women,
- Reduce child mortality,
- Combat HIV/AIDS, malaria and other diseases,
- Ensure environmental sustainability, and
- Develop a global partnership for development.

These goals were affected by corruption in different countries. The implementation of efforts of anti-corruption measures has become a serious challenge around the world. The gaps in knowledge continued to exist as regards ways of corrupt practices and the causes of it. In short diagnosis of the problem of corruption remained. The analysis of data relevant to the prevalence of corruption says it is not exclusively a problem of a particular part of the world or administrative system. It exists in different forms and pattern across the world.

unpan/un.org/intradoc/groups/public/documents/un-padm/ unpan049589-pdf 30.6.2018.

Prevention Challenges

Dealing with Complexity: In operational terms, the task of prevention is "all about intervening before the corrupt conduct occurs". Decisions about what precise action can and should be taken in a particular context are ideally based on evidence of corruption, knowledge of the context and the prevention goal to be achieved. Here an example may be referred—In Singapore a diagnosis that the relevant causes of corruption were low salaries, inefficient administrative systems. On the basis of it anti-corruption strategy may be developed, as an independent, well-resourced anti-corruption agency:

- A dynamic, monitoring strategy,
- Civil service salaries competition with private sector, and
- Reduction of red tape (Quah, 2007).

Understanding that corruption is a complex phenomenon with many forms and "faces" Campos and Pradhan suggested prevention strategies and plan that combine multiple dimensions and mechanisms with the intention of affecting incentives and opportunities for corruption and creating behaviours control.

Huberts identifies six strategies that represent the range of policy levers at the national level:

- *Economic* – emphasizes the need for the economic stimuli for corruption to be reduced and suggests that such might be achieved by paying higher civil service salaries.
- *Educational* – aims at altering the attitudes and values of the populace and civil servants alike via training and education campaigns and engagement of the media.
- *Cultural* – ensuring that the behaviour and attitudes of those in power are subject to stringent codes of conduct and their behaviour filters down to civil servants.
- *Organizational or bureaucratic* – strengthening internal control systems such as auditing to detect corrupt activity, and staff rotation to reduce the propensity for individuals to establish themselves in *entrenched* corruption.
- *Political* – increasing in transparency in terms, for example, of the monitoring of party finances and more broadly, a clearer and more definite separation of powers in terms of the judiciary and the state.
- *Judicial and repressive measures* – advocates harsher penalties for corrupt practices but also the creation of independent anti-corruption agencies.

If the purpose of prevention is to promote the integrity of government then prevention efforts have to be both positive as well as negative, capable of encouraging good behaviour as well as detecting and punishing the bad. In the 1990s Transparency International developed a model National Integrity System (NIS) comprising a set of institutions and multiple stakeholders that together support the integrity of a nation using both enforcement and enabling methods. Ideally integrity systems integrate a set of mechanisms that both reinforce desired behaviour (e.g. education, leadership, culture, decision processes) and detect impropriety.

Understanding Context: The UNCAC Technical Guide advises addressing the implementation challenge by recommending a preparatory assessment of the level of corruption vulnerability or risk in the relevant context—that identifies the trends, causes, types, pervasiveness and seriousness or impact of corruption. This will help develop a better knowledge of the activities and sectors exposed to corruption, and the basis for the development of a preventive strategy, buttressed with relevant policies and practices for better prevention and detection of corruption.

Many techniques for understanding the relevant organizational, sectoral or national context can be incorporated into a risk analysis regardless of the particular process used. Standard research methods such as surveys, literature reviews, case studies and analysis of allegations and comparative methodology can be used to expose the performance audits can enable learning from specific corrupt events.

Continuous Adjustment: In the face of dynamic character of context of corruption continuous effort is needed to both evaluate the effectiveness of prevention measures and to gather intelligence about the drivers or enablers of corruption in the context. With these information efforts can be monitored and adjusted to perform better, demonstrate their effectiveness and build public trust. Understanding "what works best under what conditions" will help us to know "what the right mix of corruption control is under specific circumstances" may lead to additional theories on the causes of corruption. Alternative explanations and understanding of corruption in particular countries can help us reconsider the effectiveness of existing policy instruments to combat corruption. (Graaf, 2007).

Effectiveness of Legal Frameworks: Corruption has been the subject of legal prohibitions for centuries. In anti-corruption terms a state's legal systems play a unique role in raising awareness by authoritatively articulating undesirable conduct, and in their potential to deter corrupt conduct by prosecuting and imposing penalties. The behaviours traditionally targeted by corruption offences were bribery and actions that equated improper public official behaviour misconduct in public office or breach of public trust. The range of specific types of corrupt behaviours now includes those required to be criminalized by the United Nations Convention Against Corruption (UNCAC): bribery, embezzlement, influence peddling, abuse of office, illicit enrichment, and money laundering (UNODC 2004). Breaches of electoral law, lobbying regulation, post-separation employment and mandatory disclosure rules can also be dealt with in administrative legal instruments such as civil service laws or codes that govern the employment of public officials.

In 2001 the World Bank reported that because "enacting an anti-corruption law is a speedy, inexpensive way to start addressing" corruption prospective anti-corruption laws had "proliferated throughout the developed world" (World Bank, 2001). The problems associated with using legal prohibitions as a quick fix can lead to non-compliance and the diversion of effort away from "more fundamental and systemic governance reforms" (Kaufman, 2003).

A more nuanced use of legislation was suggested by an analysis of the failure of anti-corruption laws in central and eastern Europe. It recommended a more "target centred" approach that would "raise awareness among target groups, take existing social norms into account, and rely on positive incentives as well as, or rather than, increasing penalties' and repealing or amending failed laws so as to undermine the credibility of the legal system by chronic non-compliance or non-enforcement (Batory 2012).

Anti-corruption agencies (ACAs), where they exist are usually part of the law enforcement framework. Since 1990s, more than 30 countries have established some form of ACA (Meagher and Voland, 2006) and many have used the ACA model to comply with UNCAC (Hassman *et. at*, 2009).

ACA models vary between a "one stop" ACA that both investigates and prosecutes corrupt conduct and one that investigates but relies on the independent criminal prosecution service to achieve convictions of corrupt perpetrators. The intention behind the latter is to reduce the layers of bureaucracy, to impose an accountability mechanism on the ACA and to encourage prosecuting bodies to take the responsibility for their own integrity. The risk in this model is that an effective ACA could be undermined by corruption or incompetence in the prosecution service which could public support for the ACA especially if its performance is measures by successful prosecutions.

The prosecution of offences can present challenges that are highly context-dependent. Where ACAs have a prosecutorial as well as an investigative and preventive role, dependence on a functioning legal system is not as critical but the risk arises that an ACA could become unaccountable or disputes over jurisdiction could arise.

Prosecutions can also be impeded by jurisdictional disputes if corruption and misconduct are subject to more than one legal framework. Managing the potential for criminal, administrative and employment laws to conflict, overlap or delay the imposition of non-legal penalties and enforcement frameworks is essential for maintaining the effectiveness and credibility of an anti-corruption strategy.

Institutional Effectiveness: Corruption has often been described as evidence of institutional failure. In the case of public administration, we talk of failure of government departments or agencies. Corruption risk factors have been identified in relation to the structure and processes, administrative capacity and the culture of public administration.

The structural effect of the public sector reforms of the 1980s that introduced competition, focus on results over process, prioritize responsiveness to elected officials and govern with "market-type-mechanism" has segregated modern public administration from the traditional public service corps into smaller offices, agencies, authorities and business units. The external boundaries of the institutions of public administration have been reduced or shifted with privatization, outsourcing and introduction of competitive business practices and the need for public-private interaction has increased and consequently the opportunities for corruption.

Ensuring accountability of public services delivered by semi-privatized entities, outsourced providers services and contracted staff can be more difficult and expensive. The contract services have introduced new set of risks from contractor's opportunism, reduced public accountability, dissonant values etc. (Mills, 2002).

Opportunities for corruption can emerge in the environment if an organization's processes have not kept up with its structural changes. Public officials who are expected to be responsive, innovative in service delivery and achieve productivity gains to reduce government spendingmay no longer have available to them the processes that accompanied the traditional structures and acted as controls on improper conduct. Hierarchical supervision, document-based management and control by standardized rules have been replaced by increased managerial discretion, local decision making and the concentration of authority in fewer individuals.

In the new environment it is not feasible to remove individual discretion. Instead people factors have become more critical in controlling corruption risks. Managers in particular need a different and wider range of skills than in the past. Rather than rely on the rigidity of structures to control behaviour managers are expected to manage informal communication channels and to model appropriate behaviour (Waldersee, 2012).

Competence in contract management and procurement is increasingly needed as public officials work more often with suppliers, contractors and other private sector partners (OECD, 2007; ICAC, 2011B). An analysis of ICAC inquiries over the past 20 years revealed some corruption risks in commercial relationships, particularly in managing contractor relationship.

The largest category of organizational risk factors for public sector corruption found in that study involved failures of management at all levels—supervisors, middle managers and senior management. At lower levels inadequate supervision and work review practices appeared frequently in the ICAC reports as well as inadequate knowledge, skills or experience of corrupt public officials or their supervisors and managers. Typically, managers did not sufficiently understand the work to recognize that corrupt activity was happening while others facilitate the corruption by tolerating low level non-compliance with all kinds of organizational rules.

Organizational incompetence was evident in a variety of forms including the failure to monitor performance or implementation, supervise and plan strategically. The second is the way that senior managers respond to specifically ethical issues which can include behaviour—on the part of managers such as (ICAC, 1999):

- Tolerating or rewarding unethical behaviour.
- "Individual ethics, personal ambition and poor supervision".
- Not taking action about corruption and behaving inconsistently.

- Emphasizing the "bottom line" of the organization over other values.

These conditions have been said to contribute to the particular "Work Culture" of an organization that is sometimes also understood as organizational culture. Cultures exert a powerful influence on behaviour and exist in communities of all kinds. Large public institutions commonly display sub-culture and counter-cultures in their various subdivisions and outposts. For this reason, reforms such as the introduction of anti-corruption initiatives are said to work best if approached from the "bottom up" as well as "top down" (Theobald, 1997; Lambsdorff, 2008). By failing to acknowledge the existence of informal as well as formal rules and norms (Ocampo, 2000) reforms imposed without reference to local conditions, whether organizational, sectoral or national, can easily fail or worse, be counter-productive (Batory, 2012). A common organizational example is when codes of conduct are introduced without adequate preparation or support (Gilman, 2005; Brien, 2001).

At the national level an over view of governance in pacific island nations reported local challenges in implementation of governance initiatives such as lack of stakeholder's commitment, disconnection between modern government and local traditions especially in communities outside the capital cities with governance reforms seen as complex and foreign to local culture and values (ADB, 2004). Similar challenges are experienced inside organizations where parallel cultures inside organizations have their own norms and rules that can be actively hostile to anti-corruption efforts (ICAC, 2008b).

This challenge is acknowledged in the OECD tool for analyzing international drivers of corruption which is expressly intended to focus "Not just on the formal, rule-based institutions of governance but also on the informal rules of the game, the complex interactions between economic and political change, and the context specific incentives that shape political behaviour" (OECD, 2012:83). For corruption purposes it is useful to consider also that the public sector is not only an institution of the political economy. More research and analysis that acknowledge the public sector as a social and organizational entity with the capacity to influence the behaviour of those it employs and interact with.

Human Resources Practices: Many of the corruption factors that originate with individuals (the "people" factor) can be addressed to some extent by human resources policy and practices. The most longstanding in the anti-corruption literature is the question of remuneration. Early analysis maintained that increasing public sector salaries would only increase the size of bribes but the role of low salaries may be more complex. Salaries that are at least competitive with the private sector can act against corruption in several ways. First, the impoverished public official may have incentive to ask for a bribe. Second, a low paid but not impoverished public official who feels, nonetheless, aggrieved by the salary and entitled to pick up extra benefits where possible may be less inclined to do so.

A situation where aggrieved officials perceive that they are unfairly treated in the workplace in ways other than salary can also be a risk factor (Tomlinson and Greenberg, 2005; ICAC, 2008c) to be managed by human resources policy and practice that ensures fair remuneration and advancements.

An obvious reaction to corruption in public administration is to re-emphasize the professional ethics of public administration. Ethics training is recommended in the UNCAC Technical Guide and is a standard element of organizational integrity system (Paine 1994). UNCAC Article 7 also refers to the need to raise the risk awareness of public officials.

A challenge to the professional model of public administration is the growth of contractualisation in the public administration. Contract staff employed from the private sector on short-term contract may not have the benefit of training or experience of public administration. Contractors are increasingly needed for technical expertise that is not available inside the public agency increasing the risk of corruption. The corruption risk is found when supervision is inadequate and recruitment is not made with due diligence. Recruitment process and background checking combined with managers effectively communicating standards of conduct are now essential corruption controls (OECD, 2004; Waldersee).

The role of general competence as a control on corruption is not well explored in the literature but a review of NSW ICAC inquiries exposed a relevant skill deficit among managers and supervisors who were unable to detect corrupt behaviour by subordinates with more knowledge of technical processes (Mills and Cooper, 2007). Enhancing leadership by using appropriate measures in systematic performance in management is recommended (ICAC, 2008c). Incompetence is also a risk factor of corruption.

Information and Communication Technology (ICT)

Information and Communication Technologies have been hailed as the answer to practical problems of increasing transparency and public accountability in public administration. ICT can make it easier to citizens to scrutinize government activity and to voice concerns and opinions about its performance. The ICT in public administration also presents two types of corruption prevention challenges.

- The first is the appearance of fraudulent activity in public administration. It is more easy as well as more damaging by using ICT.
- The second is the more dependence of public sector agencies on ICT at the operational level. It requires technical expertise and buying of the expertize without due diligence exposes public authorities to the challenges of corruption. The core challenge is the maintaining costly expertise.

ICT plays a role in preventing corruption not only in accountability and transparency but also by supporting the quality of an organization's operational efficiency and robust internal governance. In side public sector agencies electronic records management systems can improve the quality, reliability—and even the existence of public records and administrative performance generally. Electronic data can also facilitate more efficient auditing and *ex-poste* investigation of processes and analysis of corruption risks that can be used as strategic intelligence to improve systems.

Citizen Engagement

- *Scrutiny*: The role of citizens in preventing corruption is based on both the principles of accountability of the public administration and the practical power external scrutiny to achieve it. The theory is that if public officials are less likely to act corruptly if they are being observed and may have to explain their actions. The policy levers for public scrutiny may be legal. The media have traditionally been seen as leaders in facilitating public scrutiny of government activities.

- *Trust in government*: Increased contact between public officials and members of the public goes beyond the threat of scrutiny and deterrence to enhance the level of trust between public administration and citizens with benefits of both for effectiveness of government and anti-corruption investigations (Langseth, 2001).
- *Information and awareness*: Citizens will not be inclined to scrutinize or report corrupt behaviour if they do not recognize it as wrong. In the conventional anti-corruption agency (ACA) model, the third core function is to educate the public the harm of corruption.

Indian Scenerio of Anti-Corruption Effort: After the transfer of power, the new popular Government took charge of administration of the country in an atmosphere surcharged with patriotism and high ideals. In spite of the fact that the new Governments faced with grave problems caused by partition of the country, heavy responsibility of running administration with many vacant responsible positions occupied by British officials during pre-Independence period the Governments exhibited commendable enthusiasm to tackle the problem of corruption.[8]

During Second World War the administration of India was seriously ailed by the problem of corruption in public service, especially the War and Supply Departments were heavily infected by this germ of corruption. In 1941 the Government of India constituted Special Police Establishment to investigate the cases of bribery and corruption in the transactions with the War and Supply Departments. After one year, i.e. in 1942, the Department of Railways was brought to the jurisdiction of the Special Police Establishment. In 1946 the Delhi Police Establishment Act was passed by which the Delhi Police Establishment was transferred to the Home Department which was later known as the Ministry of Home Affairs and its jurisdiction was extended to all States and

Union Territories. In 1953, an Enforcement Wing was added to the Delhi Special Police Establishment to tackle the offences relating to breach of import and export regulations.[9] The Prevention of Corruption Act became law on 11th March, 1947. Under this Act a public servant is said to commit the offence of criminal misconduct if:

(a) He habitually accepts or obtains and agrees to accept or attempts to obtain from any person for himself or for any other person, any gratification (other than legal remuneration) as a motive or reward;
(b) He habitually accepts or obtains and agrees to accept or attempts to obtain from any person for himself or for any other person, any valuable thing without consideration or for considertion which he knows to be inadequate from a person having connection with the official functions of himself or of any public servant to whom he is subordinate;
(c) He dishonestly or fraudulently misappropriates or otherwise converts for his own use any property entrusted to him or under his control as a public servant or allows any other person so to do;
(d) He by corrupt or illegal means or by otherwise abusing his position as public servant, obtains for himself or for any other person so to do; and
(e) He or any person on his behalf is in possession or has, at any time during the period of his office, been in possession, for which the public servant cannot satisfactorily account, of pecuniary resources or property disproportionate to his known sources of income.

Again in 1988 the Prevention of Corruption Act was passed by the Parliament of India to combat corruption in government agencies and public sector business in India. Under this Act following are the offences along with the punishments for them:

(a) Taking gratification in order to influence public servant, by corrupt or illegal means, shall be punishable with imprisonment for a term which shall not be less than three years. It may also be extended to seven years and may be liable to fine.

(b) Taking gratification, for exercise of personal influence with public servant shall be punishable with imprisonment for a term which shall not be less than six months but may be extended to five years and shall also be liable to fine;
(c) Abetment by public servant of offences defined in the Act (Section 8 or 9) shall be punishable with imprisonment for a term which shall not be less than six months but may be extended to five years and shall also be liable to fine.
(d) Public servant obtaining valuable thing without consideration from person concerned in proceeding or business transacted by public servant, shall be punishable with imprisonment for a term which shall not be less than six months but may be extended to five years and shall also be liable to fine.
(e) Punishment for abetment of offences defined in the Act (Sections 7 and 11) shall be punishable with imprisonment for a term which shall not be less than six months but may be extended to five years and shall also be liable to fine;
(f) Any public servant, who commits criminal misconduct shall be punishable with imprisonment for a term of not less than one year but which may be extended to 7 years and shall also be liable to fine; and
(g) Habitual committing of offence under (Sections 8, 9, 12) shall be punishable with imprisonment for a term which shall be not less than 2 years but may be extented to 7 years and shall also be liable to fine.

The Act empowered the Central and the State governments to appoint special Judges by notifying in the Official Gazette, to try the following offences:

(a) Any offence punishable under the Act of 1988;
(b) Any consipiracy to commit or any attempt to commit or any abetment of any of the offences specified under the Act.

As regards the qualification of the special judge the Act says that he should be or should have been a Session Judge or an Additional Session Judge or Assistant Session Judge under the Code of Criminal Procedure, 1973.[10]

In short the 1988 Prevention of Corruption Act incorporates corruption in the public and private sectors in the form of active and passive bribery, extortion, bribery of foreign officials, abuse of office and money laundering.[11]

On 9th August, 2018 The Prevention of Corruption (Amendment) Act, 2018 was enacted. The objective of the amendments was to undertake preventive measure in line of global standards of anti-bribery and anti-corruption measures. For example, if any party contracting with a company indulges in corrupt practices and the company accepts it for lack of procedures or guidelines in place, which could otherwise prevented it, then the company (and its Directors) could get prosecuted under the Act.[12]

Another effort of the Governnment is the Prevention of Money Laundering Act, 2002 (amended in 2005). Under this Act whosoever directly or indirectly attempts to indulge or knowingly assists or knowingly is a party or is actually involved in any process or activity connected proceeds of crime including concealment or use and projecting or claiming as untainted property shall be guilty of offence of money laundering. Any person who commits the offence of money laundering shall be punishable with rigorous imprisonment for a term of three years and may be extened to seven years and he mal also be liable to fine.[13]

The Right to Information (RTI) Act, 2005 may be considered as contry's most critical achievments in the fight against corruption in recent years. Under this Act, any citizen may request information from a "public authority" which is required to reply expeditiously or within 30 days. The Act also requires every public authority to computerize their records for wide dissemination and to proactively publish certain categories of information for easy citizen access.[14]

The Bakshi Tek Chand Committee under the chairmanship of BakshiTek Chand, retired Judge of the Lahore High Court was set up in 1949 to review the working of the Prevention of Corruption Act, 1947 to make recommendations with regard to any improvement that might be considered necessary in the laws as well as in regard to the machinery for enforcing them, to assess the extent of success achieved by the Special Police Establishment in combating corruption and to make recommendations regarding continuance, strengthening etc. The Railway Corruption Inquiry Committee under the Chairmanship of Acharya Kripalani was appointed in October 1953. The Administrative Vigilance Division was set up in August 1955 and the vigilance units in the Ministries/ Departments came into being. The Vivian Bose Commission was appointed in December 1956.[15]

In April 1963 the Central Bureau of Investigation was created and the Special Police Estabishment was made one of its units.

While discussing the efforts of the Government of India to prevent corruption in administration one has to appreciate the strong steps taken by Lal Bahadur Shastri, who was the Prime Minister of India for a very short period after demise of Jawaharlal Nehru, the first Prime Minister of India. On 6th June, 1962 on the floor of Lok Sabha several Members of Parliament pointed out the menace of corruption in administration while discussing the Demands for the Ministry of Home Affairs. At that time Lal Bahadur Shastri was the Minister for Home Affairs. In reply to it Shastri said:

> "I feel that this matter should not be entirely left for consideration in the hands of officials. It is desirable that there should be exchange of views between them and public men of experience. Perhaps, Hon. Members might have read in the papers that I have suggested that a formal Committee should consider the important aspects of the evils of corruption. But I do not want to make it a formal Committee as such and wait for its report. Since we know most of the problems, the real point is to take remedial action. I, therefore, propose to request some Members of Parliament and, if possible, other public men to sit with our own officers in order to review the problem of corruption and make suggestions."

Thus for the first time emphasis was given by Lal Bahadur Shastri to involve public men of experince in the process of eradicating corruption in adminsitration.

On the basis of the statement of Lal Bahadur Shastri on the

floor of Lok Sabha the Government of India constituted a Committee with the following members:

1. K. Santhanam, MP Chairman
2. Santosh Kumar Basu, MP Member
3. Tika Ram Paliwal, MP Member
4. R.K. Khadilkar, MP Member
5. Nath Pai, MP Member
6. Shambu Nath Chaturvedi, MP Member
7. L.P. Singh, Director Administrative Vigilance Division, Member
8. D.P. Kohli, IGP, Special Police Establishment. Member Joint Director, Administrative Vigilance Division, Secretary (T.C.A. Ramanujachari).

Terms of References Were

- To examine the organization, set-up, functions and responsibilities of the Vigilance Units in the Ministries and Departments of Government of India and to suggest measures to make them more effective.
- To examine the organization, strength, procedures and methods of work of the Special Police Establishment and the difficulties experienced by it, and to suggest measures to further improve its working.
- To consider and suggest steps to be taken to emphasize the responsibilities of each Department for checking corruption.
- To suggest changes in law which would ensure speedy trial of cases of bribery, corruption and criminal misconduct, and make the law otherwise more effective.

To examine the rules relating to disciplinary proceedings and to consider what changes are necessary in order to expedite these proceedings and to make them more effective.

- To suggest measures calculated to produce a social climate both amongst public servants and in the general public in which bribery and corruption may not flourish.
- To examine the Government Servants' Conduct Rules and

to recommend changes necessary for ensuring maintenance of absolute integrity in the public services.

- To suggest steps for securing public support for anti-corruption measures.
- To consider special measures that may be necessary in corporate public undertakings to secure honesty and integrity amongst their employees.

With these terms of references, the Santhanam Committee held its first meeting on 10th September, 1962 and since then it held 87 sittings till the finalization of its report. The Committee studied comprehensively the systems of anti-corruption machineries available in different countries. It was also successful to secure cooperation of two important divisions of administration, Administrative Vigilance Division and Delhi Special Police Establishment which prepared quite a good number of background papers on the issue. These included, system of Ombudsman in Scandinavian countries, the Office of the Procurator in the Communist countries and the systems prevalent in other countries for dealing with complaints of citizens against administration and their redress. Briefs were prepared on the modes, extent and scope for corruption in the more important Ministries/Departments and other Ancillary matters. The Indian Law Institute also extended its help by preparing a note on the law relating to corruption in the countries like UK, USA, Pakistan, Canada, Burma, Ghana and France.

The Committee members also visited Bangalore, Kolkata (Calcutta), Mumbai (Bombay) to study the problems of corruption in relation to public undertakings, import/export controls, income-tax, excise and customs, and in all these places met representatives of commercial and other institutions, and prominent individuals.

It also examined several witnesses including two Central Ministers, two Chief Ministers, two State Ministers, some Secretaries to Government of India, members of the Central Board of Revenue, Commissioners of Income Tax, General Managers of Zonal Railways, and senior officers of the Vigilance Departments and of the Delhi Special Police Establishment. They also secured opinions of journalists, public men and retired administrators and many others.[16]

The Santhanam Committee suggested amendment of the

Article 311 of the Constitution so as to make the judicial processes in corruption cases easy and speedy; there should be Central Vigilance Commission with autonomous powers; that the Government Servants' Conduct Rules should be amended restricting the employment of retired Government servants by private businessmen.

The Government considered the recommendations of the Santhanam too far-reaching and rejected them in part. Instead of Statutory Commission of high officials, the Government has set up a Commission of non-officials.

Following the recommendations of the Santhanam Committee the Government of India strengthened the Special Police Establishment by entrusting more powers. The wing of the Specal Police Establshment dealing with mal-practces and offences occurring in connection with the management of of joint stock companies and infringment of export-import regulations, was expanded and strengthened to take up cases of breaches of foreign exchange regulations and importane cases of smuggling, evasion of custom duty, under-invocing and over-invoicing. With a view to extend and intensify the anti-corruption activities.

There existed two types of vigilance machineries at the epartmental level—one, the Administrative Vigilance Division in the Ministry of Home Affairs and the other, Vigilance Units in the respective Ministries and Departments and their counterparts at the public undertakings. The Administrative Vigilance Division was set up in August 1955 with a view to assuming overall responsibility and providing the necessary drive and vigorous action by the individual Ministries and Departments. However, the main responsibilityfor vigilance and action lies with the Secretaries and Heads of the Ministries and Departments respectively. But the Santhanam Committee felt that the existing vigilance machinery was inadequate to deal with the problem effectively. It suggested for establishment of a Central Vigilance Commission. According to the Santhanam Committee the Commission would have three Directorates, viz, Directorate General, Complaints and Redress, Central Police Organization and Directorate of Vigilance. The Chief Executive is to be appointed by the President in the same manner as the Comptroller and Auditor General. He is to hold office for six years or until he attains the age of 65 and on ceasing to hold office, he is to be ineligible for any further government office.

His status is to be that of the Secretary to the Government without being subordinate to any Ministry.

However, the Government rejected the recommendation on the ground that it was too far-reaching. Instead of a Statutory Commission of high officials, the Government set up a Commission of non-officials. The Chairman of the Commission is a retired senior administrative officer of the ICS rank and besides the Chairman, there are six part-time members, five of them being members of Parliament and sixth of them an ex-civil servant. The Commission has the power of investigation of corruption cases.

NOTES

1. https://www.google.com/search?q=Speech+by=Wolfensohn+Cancer+of+corruption& rlz=kicHBD.enINBIINB dt.21/1/2019
2. https://www.nvestpedia.com/terms/o/oecd.asp dt. 29.6.2018
3. https://en.wikipedia.org/wiki/OECD_Anti-Bribery_Convention dt. 4.1.2019.
4. https://www.oecd.org/daf/anti-bribery_recommendation_brief.pdf. dt 6.1.2019.
5. https://www.unodc.org/southasis/enfrontpage/2011.may/indian-govt-ratifies-two-un-conventions.html date. 18.6.2018.
6. https://www.google.com/search?q=united=nations+convention+against+ corruption&riz=ICICIN8IIIN8II dt. 11.1.2029.
7. https://times of India.indiatimes.com/india/6-years-after-signig-india-yet-to-ratify-UN-Conv. Date 18.6.2018.
8. cvc,nic.in/sites/default/files/ault/scr_rpt_cvc.pdf 4.8.2018.
9. Tyagi, A.R. (1989), *Public Administration*, Atma Ram & Sons; Delhi.
10. https://wikipedia.org/wiki/Prvention_or_Corruption_Act_1988 dt. 28.12.2018.
11. http://www.preserverarticles.com/2012031427266/what-are-the-causes of administrative-corruption-in-india.html dt. 27.12.2018.
12. www.mondaq.com/index/x/726890/white+collar+crime+Fraud/the+Prevention+Corruption+Amendments dt. 29.12.2018.
13. www.enforcementdirectorate.gov.in/Prevention of Moneylaundering Act2002.pdf??P1=117281489017600032. dt. 30.12.2018.
14. http://www.preserve articles.com/20120314272666/what-are-the-causes-of-administrative-corruption-in-india.html
15. cvc,nic.in/sites/default/files/ault/scr_rpt_cvc.pdf 4.8.2018.
16. Report of the Santhanam Committee on Prevention of Corruption 1962.

III
Ombudsmanic System in India

Every modern organization has a separate mechanism to redress the grievances of the employees and the complaints against its functioning by other people. This mechanism is generally known as Ombudamanic system. In India also provision has been made for Lokpal and Lokayukta institutions. *Lokpal* and *Lokayukta* are Sanskrit words. *Lok* means people and *Pala*, caretaker or Protector. Similarly, *Lokayukta* means Civil Commissioner. Both are anti-corruption mechanisms on the line of the Ombudsman system.

Ombudsman is a Scandinavian institution originated in 1809 itself. This institution was in dark for a long time due to various reasons like, language and geographical isolation, prevalence of colonial systems in most countries of the world etc. Only after 1950s it could draw the attention of the nations of the world as grievance redressal machinery. It was possible due to liberalisation of the countries from foreign bondage, mobolization of the people in its favour by the scholars through their writings, organization of seminars and conferences at internatinal level and ultimately, due to the efforts of the UNO to make people aware of the need of grievance redressal machinaries at the national level.

Definition: The word "OMBUDSMAN" is derived from the word "OMBUD," a Swedish word. It did not refer to complaints handling mechanism in the beginning. It indicated a spokesman or representative of another person or group of persons. Various efforts were made by some institutions and eminent persons to maintain uniformity in the usages of the term. Of these the most important is the Ombudsman Committee of the International Bar Association. This Committee suggested that the term refers to the grievance handling mechanism which comes within the scope of the following definition:

> "An Ombudsman institution is an office provided for, by the Constitution or by the action of the Legislature or Parliament and headed by the independent, high level public official who receives complaints from aggrieved persons against Government agencies, officials, and employees or who acts on his own motion and who has the power to investigate, recommend corrective action and the issue reports."

Origin: The Swedish Constitution created the office of Ombusdman in 1809 itself as the watch-dog of the Parliament against the royal officers. It remained as unique feature of Swedish administration. It was adopted by another Scandinavian country—Finland in 1919, a country with close historical ties with Sweden. Norway became another Scandinavian country to set up an Ombudsman scheme to deal with military affairs in 1952. The institution found its third and historically most important adoption by Denmark. Norway appointed Ombudsman for civil affairs in 1962 the same year New Zealand became the first Commonwealth country to adopt the Ombudsman institution. Since 1962, a large number of the countries set up similar type of institutions, for instance, Australia, Canada, Fiji, France, Great Britain, Guyana, India, Israel, Northern Ireland and Switzerland. In the U.S. there were Ombudsman officials in the States of Hawaii, Nebraska, Iowa, New York and Washington. By 1977, Ombudsman or ombudsman like institutions existed in as many as twenty five countries. Besides, in the countries like Bangladesh, Philippines and Greece, provisions pertaining to the establishment of Ombudsman like institutions have been incorporated in their respective Constitutions.

Surprisingly enough, in spite of all kinds of social, economic, legal, constitutional, political, administrative, demographic and ecological diversities prevalent in different parts of the world almost all the countries favoured the Ombudsman institution. India is not an exception. India is also making attempts to introduce this Ombudsmanic system to redress the grievances of the people. The term Lokpal was coined in 1963 by Laxmi Mall Singhvi, a member of Parliament during a pariamentary debate on grievance redressal mechanism.

Why Ombudsman: The citizens of a democratic country in the modern world have realized the necessity of effective handling of their grievances by the Government. Mere enumeration of Human Rights in the Constitution, the Charter, the Declaration and the Laws cannot protect the Human Rights. These can be ably protected by the effective machineries to redress the grievances of the people. The Ombudsman is one of the institutions essential to a democratic society. Barnard Frank identifies the reasons for the desirability of the Ombudsman institution as follows:

First, the modern state is a Welfare State. The functions of the Welfare State are unlimited. It covers each and every aspect of human life. It has extensive powers and discretion in the formulation of policies affecting a man from birth to death. Extensive powers and discretion have been granted to the Government Departments and their allied agencies. As a consequences, there is a wide scope of friction between the citizens and the officials. Protection of the individuals has become the fundamental requirement against the executive and administrative mistakes and abuse of powers. This has become a great concern of the citizens of both developed and developing countries.

What Barnard has said is no doubt true with the transformation of the Police State to the Welfare State. It may be added that today the state like India is more than a Welfare State. It has to play the role of an innovator to invent new techniques or ways for the progress of the society in the fast changing situation brought by the progress of science and technology and the appeal of world leadership in different fronts to the nations to participate in the decisions for the progress of world humanity, like, 'Health For All', Education For All' etc. Under such situation the very process of administrative system has already under changes and some are yet to be changed. Naturally, the new form of grievances will arise and similar nature of grievances will arise in different areas. This requires separate independent mechanism to redress the grievances of the citizens.

Second, the activities of bureaucracy are not only increasing in number but also becoming more complex and comprehensive in nature. This trend compels people to reemphasize their legal rights which invites additional protection by separate mechanism.

Third, one of the important functions of the legislature is the supervision of the administration. Extensive delegation of the power to the bureaucracy makes legislative supervision inadequate. This inadequacy can be made up with the introduction of Ombudsman institution.

Fourth, the complaint-handling role is played by the legislators also. One of the earliest scholarly references to this is found in the work of political anthropologists F.G. Bailey.

The term Lokpal was coined in 1963 by Laxmi Mall Singhvi, a member of Parliament during a parliamentary debate on grievance redressal mechanism suggestions were made to redress the grievances of the people through Scandinavian Ombudsmanic system. The eminent persons (Legal Luminaries) like M.C. Setalvad, L.M. Singhvi insisted creation of this institution in India. The existence of widespread inefficiency and the un-responsiveness of administration to popular needs caused formation of Administrative Reforms Commission by the Government of India. It was requested to consider, among other matters, problem of redress of citizens' grievances keeping in mind the need for ensuring the highest standards of efficiency and integrity in the public services and also for making public services responsive to the people.

It was realized by the advocates of the Ombudsmanic system, especially by Rowat that for populous, federal, racially heterogeneous or developing countries like India, there was a need of a Commission of three or more members, which might be called the Ombudsman. The Commissioners would decide minor cases individually but important cases together. Each could specialize in a particular area or type of administration. The Commission could include a judge and an experienced administrator. In this context of Commonwealth countries, the growing Cabinet domination of Parliament is an additional argument for the appointment of such an officer, who should be accountable only to Parliament, should be appointed on a non-partisan basis for a long term, and should be removable by Parliament, and whose jurisdiction should extend to all administrative authorities and to the highest officials in the land. Professor Rowat was also careful to indicate that while introducing this system one must keep in mind:

> "It (Ombudsman) cannot be a panacea. A number of people seem to regard "Ombudsman" as a kind of magic word that will cure all the administrative ills. But the age-old problem of the relation between the state and the individual is far too complex to be solved by one simple scheme. We need a whole variety of controls over administrative action, and the ombudsman scheme must be accompanied by a number of other reforms that are needed to fill the gaps in our system."[1]

On 5th January, 1966 The Administrative Reforms Commission was set up by Government of India under the chairmanship of Morarji R. Desai with five other members. The chairman resigned on his appointment as Deputy Prime Minister of the Government of India. Later K. Hanumanthaiya became the chairman and other members were H.V. Kamath, D. Mookherjee, V. Shankar and T.N. Singh. The Commission was entrusted the responsibility to "give consideration to the need for ensuring the highest standards of efficiency and integrity in the public services, and for making public administration a fit instrument for carrying out the social and economic policies of the Government and achieving social and economic goals of development, as also one which is responsive to the people."[2]

In its report submitted on 20th October, 1966 recommended appointment of a Lok Pal at the centre and a Lok Ayukta in each state to inquire into allegations of corruption and mal-administration against Union Ministers and Secretaries. While recommending the creation of such institutions the Commission stated, "the special circumstances relating to our country can be fully met by providing for the redress of citizens' grievances. There should be one authority dealing with complaints against the administrative acts of Ministers of Secretaries to Government at the Union and in the States. There should be another authority in each State and at the Centre for dealing with complaints against the administrative acts of other officials. All these authorities should be independent of the executive as well as the legislature and the judiciary. The authority dealing with the complaints against the Ministers and Secretaries to government may be designated Lokpal, while the authorities at the Centre and in the States empowered to deal with complaints other officials may be designated Lokayukta."

The Commission also pointed out clearly that the administration itelf must play the major role in reducing the area of grievances and providing remedies wherever necessary and feasible. For this purpose there should be established in each Ministry or Department, as the case may be, suitable machinery for the receipt and investigation of complaints and for providing remedies. The responsibility of the Departments to deal with public grievances must squarely be faced by them in the first instance.

Lokpal: President of India shall appoint Lokpal by warrant under his hand and seal in consultation with the Chief Justice of India and the Leader of the Opposition in Lok Sabha, if there be no such Leader, then a person has to be elected bythe members of the Opposition in Lok Sabha in the manner directed by the Speaker for the purpose.

Conditions for appointment: The person to be appointed should not be a member of any legislature in the country, nor hold any office of trust or profit (other than Lokpal and Lokayukta), nor connected with any political party, nor engaged in any business or profession once he enters upon his office.

Terms of office: (a) the tenure of Lokpal will be five years from the date he takes over his duties; (b) on ceasing to hold office, Lokpal is ineligible for further employment (whether as Lokpal or Lokayukta or in any other capacity) under the Government of India or under the Government of a State or in/under any local authority or corporation owned or controlled by Central Government or Government company or society; (c) pay, pension and allowances – the Lokpal shall get a salary of Rs. 5,000 per month. As regards pension and other allowances these will be determined as per that of Chief Justice of India; and (d) Removal, subject to the provision of Article 311, Lokpal can be removed from his office by President of India on the ground of misbehaviour or incapacity and on no other ground, the inquiry required to be held under clause (2) of Article 311 has to be held by a serving or retired Judge of Supreme Court appointed for the purpose by the President and the report of inquiry to be placed before both the Houses of Parliament by the President.

Scope of functions: Lokpal cannot conduct any investigation in the case of a complaint involving grievance or allegation in respect of action taken:

(a) In a matter certified by a Secretary as affecting relations or dealings between Central Government and any foreign government or any international organization of States or Government;
(b) Under Extradition Act, 1962 or Foreigners Act, 1946;
(c) For purpose of investigation of crime or protecting the security of the State including action in respect of passport and travel documents;
(d) In exercise of powers to determine whether a matter shall go to a court or not;
(e) In matters arising out of terms of contract of purely commercial nature with customers/suppliers except where harassment or gross delay in meeting contractual obligations is involved;
(f) In respect of appointment, removal, pay, discipline, super annuation or other matters relating to conditions of service of public servants; and
(g) In respect of grant of honours and awards.

Lokayukta: President shall appoint one or more than one Lokayukta in consultation with Lokpal. He will be under the administrative control of Lokpal. However, Lokpal will have no authority to question any finding, conclusion or recommendation of Lokayukta. Lokayukta will have jurisdiction over actions of public serants other than those within the purvew of Lokpal.

The conditions of appointment, terms of office, removal, scope of functions, manner of making complaints etc. will be identical to those of Lokpal.[3] In May 1968, the Lokpal and Lokayukta Bill was introduced in Lok Sabha, where it was passed on 20th August, 1969 and then sent it to Rajya Sabha for consideration. With the premature dissolution of the Lok Sabha in December 1970 the bill lapsed. On 11th April, 1971 the Bill was reintroduced in the Lok Sabha. However, the Bill could not be passed in Lok Sabha. Again on 28th July, 1977, a fresh Bill was introduced in Lok Sabha and it was sent to the Joint Committee of Parliament. On 20th July, 1978 the repot of the Joint Committee was presented and once again the Bill lapsed. On 26th August 1985, a fresh Bill for the appointment of Lok Pal was introduced in Lok Sabha and the Bill met with the same fate due to the dissolution of Lok Sabha. Again a futile effort was made to pass the Bill in Lok Sabha in 1990. The Bill lapsed due to fall of National Front Government.[4]

On 9th July 1993 the Government of India constituted a Committee under the chairmanship of N.N. Vohra, the then Home Secretary, of the Government of India to collect information on the activities of crime syndicates/mafia organizations who allegedly had developed links with and were being protected by some government functionaries and political personalities. The Committee submitted its report before both the Houses of Parliament on 1st August, 1995 in which the Committee pointed out 'the nexus between the criminal gangs, police, bureaucracy and politicians" worked in various parts of the country. The existing criminal justice system, which was essentially designed to deal with the individual offences/crimes, was unable to deal with the activities of the mafia; the provisions of law in regard to economic offences were found to be weak and there were insurmountable legal difficulties in attaching/ confiscating the properties acquired through mafia activities. The report suggested setting up of nodal agency under the Ministry of Home Affairs, Government of India, to be handled directly by the Union Home Secretary, who would be assisted by one or selected officers of the Ministry for the collation and compilation of all information received from different intelligence agencies. Subsequently, an All Party meeting was held on 15th September, 1995 under the chairmanship of the then Union Home Minister, S.B. Chavan to look into the whole gamut of criminal-political nexus and the related issue of declaration of assets and liabilities by the members of Parliament and Ministers. Following were the tasks of the Committee:

1. Setting up of a Parliamentary Committee of Ethics as distinct from the Committee of Privileges which would act as a guardian on the activities of the members of Parliament.
2. Adoption of a Code of Conduct at the level of political parties to ensure a cleaner public life, e.g. not give party tickets persons having criminal records.
3. All political parties should have open audited accounts which must be published annually.

4. Giving more teeth to the Nodal group set up on the recommendation of the Vohra Committee.
5. Changes in the legal system, simplification of the procedure and dispensation of quick justice.[5]

In 2005 the Right to Information Act was passed and it helped the civilians to move effectively for dealing with the problem of corruption. Under this Act the Indian citizens can make request to get information from the public authority. The public authority must reply within thirty days. The citizens have the opportunity to uncover the corrupt activities politicians and bureaucrats. However, this process results aggressive attitude towards the citizens who uncover corrupt activities of public personnel.

In the years immediately preceding the anti-corruption movement in 2011 there were several notable examples of alleged corruption in country. In included Adarsh Housing Society Scam, Housing Loan Scam in 2010, Radia Tapes Controversy and 2G Spectrum case etc. in February 2011 the Supreme Court of India issued order to all trial courts in the country to expedite handling of corruption cases of India. Pratibha Devi Singh Patil, President of India declared that measures to ratify the UN Convention Against Corruption and other legislative and administrative measures necessary to improve transparency would be taken. A month later, Chief Vigilance Commissioner, P.J. Thomas was forced to resign on charges of corruption by the Supreme Court. The Indian anti-corruption movement gained momentum on 5th April, 2011, when Anna Hazare began a hunger strike at Jantar Mantar in New Delhi. The main aim of the movement was to alleviate corruption in the Indian Government through introduction of the Jan Lokpal Bill. Another aim spearheaded by Ramdev was the repatriation of black money from Swiss and other foreign banks.

Anna Hazare demanded a Joint Committee comprising members of the Government and the civil society to draft the anti-corruption legislation. Manmohan Singh, then Prime Minister of India rejected the demand. Anna Hazare started hunger strike on 5th April, 2011. His strike attracted considerable support, including prominent representatives of opposition political parties including Bharatiya Janata Party and Communist Party of India.

Protest in sympathy with Anna Hazare spread to several Indian cities including Banglore, Mumbai, Chennai and Ahmedabad.

Prominent figures from Bollywood, sports and business extended their support. On 9th April, 2011 Government agreed to constitute a Joint Committee. The Committee would be headed by a politician chairperson, Pranab Mukharjee and activist non-political person as co-chairman, Shanti Bhushan. Shanti Bhushan was one of the originaal drafters of the Lokpal and Lokayukta Bill along with Justice N. Santosh Hegde, advocate Prashant Bhushan and RTI activist Arvind Kejriwal.[6]

Ultimately, the Lokpal and Lokayukta Act, 2013, commonly known as The Lokpal Act was passed by the Parliament. It is an anti-corruption Act of India which seeks to provide for establishment of the institution of Lokpal to inquire into allegations of corruption against certain public functionaries and for matters connecting them.[7]

The Bill was tabled in the Lok Sabha on 22nd December, 2011 and was passed by the House on 27th December as The Lokpal and Lokayukta Bill, 2011. It was subsequently tabled in the Rajya Sabha on 29th December. After a long debate that stretched until midnight of the following day, the vote failed to take place for lack of time. On 21st May, 2012, it was referred to a Select Committee of the Rajya Sabha for consideration. It was passed in the Rajya Sabha on 17th December, 2013 after making certain amendments to the earlier Bill and in the Lok Sabha in the next day. It received assent of President, Pranab Mukherjee on 1st January, 2014 and came into force from 16th January. The Lokpal and Lokayuktas Act 2013, commonly known as The Lokpal.

The status of the Bill in different times may be shown as below:

Year	*Cost of Lokpal (recurring)*	*Status of Bill*
1968	Rs. 300,000	The fourth Lok Sbaha dissolved before the bill passed by Rajya Sabha. The bill lapsed.
1971	Rs. 2 million	The Bill lapsed on dissolution of the Fifth Lok Sabha.
1977	Rs. 2.5 million	The Sixth Lok Sabha dissolved just before the recommendations of the Joint Select Committee could be considered.

(*Contd.*)

Year	*Cost of Lokpal (recurring)*	*Status of Bill*
1985	Rs. 2.5 million	This Bill was withdrawn by Government.
1989	Rs. 3.5 million	The Bill lapsed on dissolution of Ninth Lok Sabha.
1996	Rs.10 million	The Standing Committee presented its report to Parliament on 9th May, 1996. However, the Lok Sabha was dissolved before government could finalize its stand.
1998	Rs. 10 million	The 12th Lok Sabha was dissolved before government could take a view on the recommendations made by the Parliamentary Standing Committee.
2001	Rs. 15 million	The Lok Sabha was dissolved. Hence the bill lapsed.
2011/2012	The Government's version of Lokpal does not have any financial memorandum	Passed by the Lok Sabha. Rajya Sabha passed the Bill on 17th December, 2013. Lok Sabha passed the Bill on 18th December, 2013.

Jan Lokpal Bill: To draw the attention of the government, a focused campaign "India Against Corruption" (IAC) was started in 2011. Anna Hazare is the head of Civil Society and the IAC movement. Being a foreground for Jan Lokpal campaign till August 2011 IAC was able to upload the 23rd version of the Lokpal Bill draft. As of January 2014, the Delhi State Government led by Chief Minister, Arvind Kejriwal was preparing to adopt the Jan Lokpal Bill, but was unable to introduce it to the House.

The Jan Lokpal Bill, also known as the Citizen's Ombudsman Bill, is an anti-corruption bill drawn up by civil society activists in India seeking the appointment of a Jan Lokpal, an independent body to investigate corruption cases. This also proposes improvements to the Lokpal and Lakayukta Bill, 2011.

The Jan Lokpal aims to effectively deter corruption, compensate citizen grievances, and protect whistle-blowers. The prefix Jan (citizens) signifies that these improvements include inputs provided by "ordinary citizens" through an activist-driven, non-governmental public consultation. Kejriwal was preparing to adopt the Jan Lokpal Bill, but was unable to introduce it to the House. A comparison between draft Lokpal Bill of Government. And Jan Lokpal Bill by representatives of Anna Hazare shows the following:

(1)	(2)	(3)
Issues	Draft Lokpal Bill (Government representatives)	Draft Jan Lokpal Bill, 2011 (Nominees of Anna Hazare)
Composition	Chairperson and 10 members (at least 4 judicial members).	Chairperson and 10 members (at least 4 members with legal background) the Chairperson to have extensive knowledge of law).
Tenure	Five years or till he is 70 years of age.	Five years or till he is 70 years of age.
Manner of appointment	Presidential appointment on the recommendation of Selection Committee.	Presidential appointment on the recommendation of the Selection Committee.
Committee membership	Prime Minister, Speaker, Leader of the House of which PM is not a member, Minister of Home affairs, Leader of the Opposition in both Houses, Judge of Supreme Court, Chief Justice of a High Court, President of National Academy of Science, cabinet secretary (Secretary of Committee).	Prime Minister, Leader of Opposition in the Lok Sabha. 2 Judges of the Supreme Court, 2 Chief Justices of High Courts, the Chief Election Commissioner, the CAG, and all previous Chairpersons of Lokpal. The members shall be selected from a list prepared by the Search Committee (10 members including civil society representatives).
Qualification	Impeccable integrity with at least 25 years of experience in public affairs, academics, commerce, finance etc.	A judicial member should have held judicial office for at least 10 years or been advocate of the High Court

(Contd.)

(1)	(2)	(3)
	Once appointed, cannot be an MP, MLA or be connected with a political party, business or practice a profession. A judicial member has to be either a Chief Justice of the High Court or a Judge of the Supreme Court.	or Supreme Court for at least 15 years. All members should be of impeccable integrity with record of public service especially in the field of corruption. Must be a citizen of India at least 45 years old. Must have no case involving moral turpitude framed against him by a court. Cannot have been a government servant within the last 2 years.
Removal	Complaint against members are made to the President who may refer it to the Supreme Court who will conduct an inquiry. The President may remove the member, on the opinion of the Chief Justice, on grounds of bias, corruption, insolvency, paid employment or infirmity.	President removes members on the recommendation of the Supreme Court made within 3 months of a complaint. Grounds for removal: misbehaviour, infirmity, insolvency, paid employment outside the office. An Independent Complaints Authority at the State level inquiries into complaints against Lokpal staff.
Jurisdiction	All corruption cases under the Prevention of Corruption Act, 1988. It covers MPs, Ministers, 'Group A' officers, 'Group A' officers in a company or body owned by the government, any officer of a government-financed by society or trust or funded by Foreign Contribution (Regulation Act, 1976) or that gets funds from the public. It excludes PM, Judiciary	Offences by a public servant, including government employees, judges, MPs, Ministers, and the Prime Minister under the Indian Penal Code and the 1988 Corruption Act. Any offence committed by an MP in respect of a speech or vote in the House; wilfully giving or taking benefit from a person. Victimizing a whistle-blower or witness.

(*Contd.*)

(1)	(2)	(3)
	and any action of an MP in the Parliament or Committee.	
Investigation	Lokpal must conduct a preliminary inquiry within 30 days. If there is no *prima facie* case, the matter is closed. Given a *prima facie* case, Lokpal investigates after providing suitable forum to the accused. The investigation must be completed within six months with an optional six months extension after giving reasons in writing. No sanction shall be required by the Lokpal to investigate any complaint against a public servant.	When investigating corruption cases, the CBI works under the Lokpal. Investigation of the Prime Minister, Ministers, MPs and Judges of the Supreme Court or High Courts require the permission of a 7-member bench of the Lokpal. Investigations can last 6 to 18 months. Investigation of whistle-blower complaints who are in danger of victimization, must be completed within 3 months.
Prosecution	The Lokpal may constitute a prosecution wing headed by a director who files cases in the Special Court (to be constituted by the Central Government on recommendation of the Lokpal) Trials must complete within one year which may be extended to two years for reasons given in writing. No sanction is required to file a case against a public servant. The Lokpal files cases in the Special Court and ends a copy of the report to the competent authority. Procedure for persons other than MPS and Ministers:	The CBI's prosecution wing moves under Lokpal. After an investigation is completed, the Lokpal may either initiate prosecution against the accused or impose penalty or both. The Lokpal can initiate prosecution in the Special Court formed under the Prevention of Corruption Act, 1988. The Lokpal shall appoint retired judges or retired civil servants as judicial officers. A bench of judicial officers can impose a penalty on a public servant after conducting an inquiry. The decision shall be subject to

(*Contd.*)

(1)	(2)	(3)
	The competent authority is the Minister for officers of government bodies and the society head for officers of societies. The Lokpal recommends disciplinary proceedings to the competent authority and provides a copy of the report to the accused. The competent authority must take action within 30 days and inform the Lokpal within 6 months of initiating disciplinary proceedings. Procedure for MPs and Ministers: The competent authority is the PM for Ministers and the Lok Sabha or Rajya Sabha for MPs. The Speaker/Chairman tables the report in Parliament. The House reports to the Lokpal on any action taken within 90 days.	approval from a higher authority to be prescribed. Prosecution can be initiated against the Prime Minister, Ministers, MPs and judges of the Supreme Court or High Courts only with permission of a 7-member bench of Lokpal. If the Lokpal grants permission to investigate or initiate prosecution, no sanction is required from any authority.
Penalty	Any person making false or frivolous or vexatious complaints hall be penalized with 2 to 5 years of jail and fine of Rs. 25,000 to 2,00,000.	For any act of corruption, the penalty shall be from six months to life imprisonment. If the beneficiary for an offence is a business entity, a fine of up to five times the loss caused to the public shall be recovered. If a company director is convicted, the company shall be black-listed from any government contract. Persons making a false complaints, are fined up to Rs.1,00,00. False

(Contd.)

(1)	(2)	(3)
		complaint against a member of Lokpal may result in 3 months imprisonment.
Funding	Paid by Consolidated Fund of India.	Paid by Consolidated Fund of India. The budget of the Lokpal should not be less than 0.25 per cent of total government revenue. No sanction required from government to incur expenditure. The CAG audits Lokal and a Parliamentary Committee evaluates Lokpal operations.
Other powers	The Lokpal can search and seize documents, attach property for 90 days, file for confirming the attachment with 30 days, and recommend suspension of the accused.	The Lokpal can receive complaints from whistle-blowers, issue search warrants, attach property, recommend cancellation/modification of a lease or license or blacklist a company. If recommendation of Lokpal is not accepted, it can approach the High Court. A bench of the Lokpal can approve interception and monitoring of messages transmitted through telephone or internet.

In March 2019 for the first time in the history of the country's former Justice Pinaky Chandra Ghose was appointed as the Lokpal along with eight other members. They are former Justices of different High Courts – Justices Dilip B. Bhosale, Pradip Kumar Mahanty, Abhilasha Kumari and Ajay Kumar Tripathi. Former first woman chief of Sashatra Seema Bal, Archana Ramasundaram, ex-Maharashtra Chief Secretary Dinesh Kumar Jain, former IRS officer Mahendra Singh and Gujarat cadre ex-IAS officer Indrajeet Prasad Gautam are non-official members.

REFERENCES

1. Jain, R.B. and Jashree Pillai (1985). Article; Transplanting Ombudsman in India; *The Indian Journal of Public Administration*; July-September, Vol. XXXI No. 3.
2. Maheswari, S.R. (1988). *Indian Administration*; New Delhi: Orient Longman Private Ltd.
3. Tyagi, A.R. (1989). *Public Administration*; Delhi: Atma Ram & Sons.
4. Arora, Ramesh, K. and Rajni Goyal (1996). *Indian Public Administration*; 2nd revised edition; New Delhi: Wishwa Prakashan.
5. Indiaprosppect.org/Blog/?23 1st Apl. 2019.
6. https://www.civilserviceindia.com/subject/essay/ana-hazare-movement-against-corruption%20%html 1.4.2019.
7. https://en.wikipedia.org/wiki/the_Lokpal_and_Lokayukta_act_2013 accessed on 4.6.2018.

IV
Moral Dimension of Governance

The concept of governance cannot be divorced from its moral dimension. Every act of public servant has moral implication in addition to its financial involvement. The concepts like, 'development', 'public interest', 'welfare', 'democracy' are evolving and comprehensive concepts and all these are interlinked. Significantly, to translate the ideals behind these concepts one requires autonomy or discretionary power. The traditional hierarchical system in administration or Weberian model of bureaucratic authority may not work effectively in today's administration as it becomes complicated day by day demanding expertness or specialization in each field. Along with this demand there is also need to safeguard the moral dimension of administration.

The concept of 'development administration' is different from that of 'regular administration.' Unlike regular administration, which, to a great extent remains within the framework of rules and regulation, development administration is dynamic and innovative in nature. It is more prone to corruption. What is required under these circumstances is the honest and moral leadership to implement new policies and programmes. Because proneness towards corruption and abuse of power in different positions at the higher level of the modern administration is very high. An intelligent man who is corrupt, selfish and cruel may adopt all devices—misinterpretation of public interest and laws, involvement in unnecessary debate, non-disclosure of the fact, avoidance of responsibility etc. to hide his corrupt intention, selfish motive and cruel attitude or behaviour towards the client or public.

These will result lack of confidence of the people on the administration, emergence of unethical activities and most dangerous result is the exploitation of citizens who are the taxpayers, because every act of a civil servant has financial involvement. Here is the need of ethical accountability on the part of the service providers in a modern state. One must act at the dictate of his conscience and it will make him accountable to his own conscience. It is the main reason why education is insisted upon on the candidates to enter into public service. Lord Macaulay in 1850s itself, while asserting on the need of introduction of merit system for recruitment to the civil service pointed out that an educated man is a moral man or in other words education makes a man moral. However, today the very concept of education has been degenerated to a great extent. It becomes very fragile to enhance inner power of the individuals.

Accountability is not just in the negative sense of holding public servants responsible for their lapses. It has a positive connotation. They have the responsibility to discharge duties which are of great public significance.[1]

Moral responsibility is the status of morally deserving praise, blame, reward or punishment for an act of a man. People who have moral responsibility for an action are called moral agents.[2]

It is true that legal code cannot be identified with moral code and the state cannot dictate morality simply because morality cannot be imposed from outside. It has to be cultivated in the minds of a person. Here the state can create an environment through law for development of morality. Morality is an expression of personality, as it conceives itself to other personalities. A moral rule is a rule that a man obeys from the heart in the perspective of values he or she adhered to. In the language of MacIver, "law can no more be a substitute for morality just as the hand cannot be a substitute for the eye."[3]

Both are equally important for effective governance of a country. Since later part of the Twentieth century the moral dimension of governmental system is attracting the attention of scholars, reformers and leading public organizations at the international as well as national levels. The ethical vacuity has become prominent in politics, administration and also in the society. This trend is a serious threat to the human civilization.

The term 'Governance' refers to all processes of governing

undertaken by government and non-governmental organizations including family. However, the concept of Governance is not new. It is as old as human civilization. In most abstract sense governance is a theoretical concept referring to the actions and processes by which stable practices and organizations arise and persist. These actions and processes may operate in formal and informal organizations of any size for any purpose, good or evil, for profit or non-profit. Governance refers to a process or the act or function of exercising authority to regulate affairs of man in a given territory.

Thus, conceptually governance can be defined as an act of governing a nation or any organization or institution. As regards the concept of 'Public Governance' it is different from the concept of Government. It is something more than that of 'Government'. The term 'Government' may identify the constitutionally organized political entity having authority to rule of the nation. On the other hand the term 'Governance' identifies all the aspects of the process of policy formulation and policy implementation including the actors involved in the process. Again, the concept of good governance widens the path of understanding public administration as People's administration' with governmental initiatives and developmental interventions within the framework of philosophic, normative and ethical perspectives.[4]

Good governance is democratic governance. The normative aspect of democracy was insisted by John F. Kennedy in a statement in 1956 as, "Democracy means much more than popular government and majority rule, much more than a system of political techniques to flatter or deceive powerful blocs of voters. The true democracy, living and growing and inspiring, puts its faith in the people – faith that the people will not simply elect men who will represent their views ably and faithfully, but also elect men who will exercise their conscientious judgement – faith that the people will not condemn those whose devotion to principle leads them to unpopular courses, but will reward courage, respect them, and ultimately recognize right."[5]

While discussing the relationship between ethics and politics it is found that there were several thinkers who advocated religious and ethical basis of politics. Before Gandhi, there were several thinkers who advocated religious and ethical basis of politics. Plato in his *Republic*, Aristotle in his *Politics*, St. Augustine in his *City of God*, Sir Thomas More in his *Utopia*, and Dante in his *De*

Monarchia are prominent thinkers to underline the close relationship between ethics, religion and politics. Though Gandhi was not the original thinker on it, his originality is found in its applicability to mass politics.[6]

Greek philosopher Plato was influenced to some extent by the Pythagorianism, especially when he said justice means that each of the three elements—reason, spirit and appetite—occupies its proper place. It means hierarchically reason must be at the top and appetite at the lowest level and in-between there must be spirit in the hierarchical order. Pythagoreans spoke about harmony and justice. As regards harmony the number is very important and fundamental to it. Where there is harmony there is justice and Pythagoreans said that justice is a number. This number is a square number. In a square number there is harmony, because it is composed of equal parts. A number is a square number so long as the equality of parts is maintained. The implication of this principle is that a state is just so long as the principle of equality is maintained.[7]

The normative aspect of public administration demands the activism of human power or reasoning power of the bureaucrats. Since the bureaucrats are committed to the welfare of the society they must be able to decide what is good and what is bad at every step of their activities, especially while participating in the policy making process.[8]

Good governance is nothing but democratic governance. Dennis F. Thompson explored several ways in which public bureaucracy can be reconciled with a democratic system. Of these hierarchical model of administrative responsibility, reliance on the professionalism of the civil service to achieve responsiveness, a pluralist model of citizen involvement and participatory model are noteworthy. To Thompson participatory model is the best beginning of the reconciliation of bureaucracy and democracy.[9]

The concept 'Good Governance' has ethical or normative connotation, which helps to judge 'good' and 'bad' governance indicating certain features of it. The definition of 'Good Governance' formulated by the World Bank incorporates these features. It defined "Good Governance" as 'the one epitomized by predictable, open, an enlightened policy-making, a bureaucracy imbued with a professional ethos acting in furtherance of the public good, the rule of law, transparent processes, and a strong civil society participating in public affairs. Poor governance, on the other hand, is characterized arbitrary policy-making, unaccountable bureaucracies, enforced by unjust legal systems, the abuse of executive power, and wide spread corruption."[10]

The concept of democracy whether political or social centres round human beings. Abraham Lincoln (February 12, 1809 –April 15, 1865) the American statesman and lawyer who served as the sixteenth President of the United States of America from March 1861 until his assassination in April 1865 said, "Democracy is a government of the people, by the people and for the people". The social concept of democracy is expressed in a very simple way by Mahatma Gandhi, who led the struggle for Independence of India as, "Democracy is a Way of Life".

Both the statements indicate the worth of human beings, though both Lincoln and Gandhi conceived the ideas in two different situations—one was in the West and the other was in the East.

Nobody can deny the significance of reasoning power of a man. Because, this power justifies supremacy of man over all the animals in the world. With the help of this power he can choose the right action for the welfare of people and the progress of human civilization. This right to reason is an inherent right of each individual. Therefore, the question of grant of this right by the state or any higher authority does not arise. What is necessary is that this right has to be respected by both the ruler and the ruled. It is possible only in a democracy. In the decision making process the people take part through their representatives. On the floor of the legislature different views of the people are raised for discussion. After a threadbare discussion of different views and exchange of different ideas, decisions are taken by the members on behalf of the people whom they represent. Once a decision is taken it becomes obligatory on the part of the government to execute it whole heartedly.

In the modern democracy the people get the opportunity to participate in the decision-making process mainly through their representatives. They can also express their views through media, letters and other electronic devices. Thus, the people take part in the political process of the country. At the same time the people are required to extend cooperation at the time of implementation of the decision of the government. They must also be vigilant to see that the decision of the government is effectively implemented for achieving the goal of the policy. The citizens of a democratic country must be aware of their duties, then only self-rule is possible. They must also be prepared to face the inconveniences caused by the changes brought by the new decisions of the government. It invites self-restraint.

There is no denying the fact that arriving at a particular decision is not an easy task in a democracy. Because the views of each and every member cannot be accommodated in a decision. A decision needs to be convinced by all that it is in the interest of the society as a whole. The democratic process also requires that a consensus is to be evolved through thoughtful discussion and farsightedness, scientific analysis of each policy before finalizing it, not by manipulation, force or temptation. The differences amongst the various views of the people are not to lead to conflict and friction in the society but to resolve them in the wider perspective of the society. Democracy creates accommodative platform where dignity of the individual is respected. All these are essential for sustainable development and to keep the pace of progress of the nation.[11]

Any administrative decision is a combination of both fact and value. In fact, philosopher Bosanquet remarked, "Value is a fact at a deeper level." The problem of decision making is not merely one of expertise. It is also a problem of restoring confidence in the people. Since the articulation is absent in the people, at least the administrator has to develop a sufficiently deep value-sensitivity and skills of management of public affairs.

Decision-making, particularly at the higher levels requires not only a sharp intellectual ability to analyze problems and professional competence but emotional maturity and a deep social economic awareness which can inspire confidence and trust. Decision-making is not merely an intellectual exercise but is an amalgam of both fact and value.[12]

Democratic governance means:

- People's human rights and fundamental freedoms are respected, allowing them to live with dignity.
- People have a say in decisions that affect their lives.
- People can hold decision-makers accountable.
- Inclusive and fair-rules, institutions and practices govern social interactions.
- Women are equal partners with men in private and public spheres of life and decision-making.

- People are free from discrimination based on race, ethnicity, class, gender or any other attribute.
- The needs of future generations are reflected in current policies.
- Economic and social policies are responsive to people's needs and aspirations.
- Economic and social policies aim at eradicating poverty and expanding the choices that all people have in their lives.

Situation Leading to Emergence of the Concept of Good Governance

Since the dawn of modern democratic era in the late nineteenth century democracy has worked through nation state as a powerful force in administering a nation. Though at the initial stage democratic system worked well, gradually nation states failed to work within the framework of democratic principles. Here begins ostensibly the occurrence of democratic deficit. As people's lives become more interdependent, democratic principles of participation and equal concern for all must be reflected in the way of functioning by the new actors in the modern democracy.[13]

Experience shows that along with the entry of new actors in modern democracy administration in most states has been growing rapidly in size and complexity in recent years. This is due to the tremendous increase in its functions and authority, especially in developing countries, on account of its growing concern with the welfare and development of the people, besides the growth in the traditional functions relating to law and order, defense, tax collection, regulation and international affairs. Today citizen depends upon administration for supply of goods and services, directly or indirectly than before. This growing dependence of the individuals and families upon a big impersonal and more authoritative administration could result in rise of many occasions for tensions and conflicts between the two, leaving the former frustrated and even alienated at times.

In order to militate against undue growth of public discontent and grievances, it would be useful to undertake integrated measures for the re-organization, reorientation as well as for the increasing sensitization of the public administration. The public administration is to be recreated, renewed and revitalized.

The thrust area of such reform is to be not only in regard to organizational structures but is to be wider. An international group of public administration experts has also stressed this: "Dysfunctional and inapplicable administrative structures, systems and practices must be replaced, nothing less than dynamic organizations, resourceful management and streamlined administrative processes will suffice.....The tortuous time-consuming routines, special privileges, corruption, indolence and insolence often encumbering any governmental bureaucracies and civil services have no place in developed administration. This calls for continuous action to foster honesty and integrity and to weed out corruption, as well as to develop preventive measures." Since administrative effectiveness depends to no less extent upon the knowledge, skills, motivation and productivity of the diverse and expanding categories of the public personnel, there is also need for formulation of the progressive personnel policies in regard to recruitment, deployment, development and retention of right type of persons within the administrative systems.[14] Again, it is highly desirable to promote vigorously good human relations to subdue the rigidities of hierarchical and compartmentalized relations. The administrative culture needs to be given an increasing democratic orientation, for not only achieving better productivity within the administrative system but also for making the bureaucracy more humane in its dealings with the people.

While it is true that efficient and humanized administrative system would tend to build a good image among the people and generate less alienation and grievances among them, there is a need for positive understanding, and constructive cooperation between the two, without encouraging any tendencies towards regimentation. This could be made possible through an effective system of communication between the government administration and the people as well as through the creation of opportunities for people's association with, or participation in, decision-making and implementation within the administration.

Besides improving the efficiency of administration which would be appreciated by the citizens, politico-administrative decentralization also affords larger opportunities for their participation in the government administration. Such opportunities can be in the way of their representation on local and regional authorities entrusted with increased authority and resources in the context of the trend towards decentralization. The citizen would thus have a better understanding of government policies and programmes. This would not only strengthen legitimacy of the government but would also persuade the citizen to adopt "new ideas and practices, use the services offered," as well as "contribute their own effort and resources to the programme, give vitality to new institutions and make constructive adjustments in their lives." This is will aptly make the changes generated by development programmes more enduring. Moreover, such participation would induct more realism in Central Government's policies and programmes, as a fuller account is likely to be taken of the "local knowledge and interests". Furthermore, methods of implementation of these policies and programmes would tend to be more appropriate and elastic when these have been suggested by the local representatives of the people. Citizen's participation is also likely to provide substance and depth of durability to the impact of government programmes. Further, it would also improve local initiative and develop leadership within a locality or a community of the people.[15]

Democratic governance in this fast changing environment is about more than people having the right to vote. We have failed to realize that it must be about strengthening democratic institutions so that they keep pace with the changing distribution of economic and political power. And it must be about promoting democratic politics that make participation and public accountability possible even when the relevant power and processes lie outside the formal institutions of the state.[16]

Unfortunately, gradually the space for humanity in the global society has been narrowed down to a great extent by various inhuman activities in different parts of the world. It is a serious threat to modern democracy. Each one of us notices the disappearance of human power, emergence of unethical behaviour, domination of money power on reasoning capacity of man, bold activism of irrational elements of individuals, strong arguments in favour of undemocratic behaviour of leaders, unresponsiveness to public needs and aspirations, lack of integration between word, work and thought of modern man, multiplication of humanitarian laws in the face of disregard to human dignity and violation of human rights at every stage of man's life etc. are the very prominent indicators of degeneration of democratic principles across the world.

We have noticed that honesty, integrity, humanity etc. have been thrown out mercilessly from the modern democratic global society.

Referring to India it is said very rightly by V.R. Krishna Iyer that the ultimate authority of India's adult humanity has proved "a teasing illusion and promise of unreality' in practice, despite the categorical imperative, in Article 38 of the Constitution. The cornerstone of our democracy is fresh elections at least once in five years but the elective process has been infected by the purchasing power of the plutocracy. Elections are losing their common credibility and democratic value.[17]

Very soon the nations of the world have forgotten the situations responsible for establishment of League of Nations and United Nations of Organization followed by various other Organizations at the international and national levels as the saviors of humanity from the scourge of unthinkable barbarity and cruelty across the world.

Public services of different nations are also exposed to a new environment in the face of 'globalization', 'privatization' and 'liberalization'. Globalization may be defined differently depending on the context and on the person. Further, the precise definition of globalization is still not available. However, here mention may be made of a few definitions given by some eminent persons. Stephen Gill defines globalization as the reduction of transaction cost of transborder movements of capital and goods.[18]

Guy Brainbant says that the process of globalization not only includes opening up of world trade, development of advanced means of communication, internationalization of financial markets, growing importance of Multi-National Companies, population migration and more specifically increased mobility of workers, students, patients along with goods, capital, data and ideas is found. The term globalization also refers to the integration of economies of the world through trade and financial flows, as also through mutual exchange of technology and knowledge. Ideally, it contains inter-country movement of labour.[19]

Globalization also implies the development of local and nationalistic perspectives to a broader outlook of an interconnected and interdependent world with free transfer of capital, goods and services across national frontiers. However, it does not include unhindered movement of these.

UN defines globalization as increased and intensified flows

of goods, services, capital, ideas, information and people between countries, which produce national cross-broader integration of a number of economic, social and cultural activities.[20]

Major measures initiated as a part of the liberalization and globalization strategy in the early nineties included scrapping of the industrial licensing regime, reduction in the number of areas reserved for the public sector, amendment of the monopolies and restrictive trade practices act, start of the privatization programme, reduction in tariff rates and change over to market determined by exchange rates.[21]

Thus, Globalization briefly refers to the growing interdependence among nations compelling the sorting out of economic, social, environmental and human rights issues at the international level. It is based on the acceptance of the market forces, which intensifies international competition. It compels reconciliation of global imperatives with local needs and requirements. With this various kinds of social ailments including space for corruption also move from place to place.

Inefficiency and increased responsibility of the states due to rapid rise of expectations of the people and growth of population demanded the process to be effective and people oriented. Since privatization has a close relation to the theory of New Public Management, it encourages movement of managerial responsibility from the public to private bodies. It reduces the scope of government bureaucracy. The process of privatization provides freedom and flexibility which are generally absent in the Government control such as, Ministerial obligations, restrictions on the rights and code of conduct etc. It is expected that this freedom will enable the service providers in the private sector to maintain efficiency and flexibility in the administrative process. Due to these reasons in 1970s privatization of public services was welcomed by many European countries, Australia, New Zealand and even developing countries. India welcomes private institutions in large number in different sectors.

Once responsibility of the state is shifted to the private organizations with the assumption that people's power is being returned for effective administration, in practice it does not happen in India. These services are beyond the people's control, the government does not have effective mechanism to ensure accountability of the private service providers, in ultimate analysis most of these organizations are guided only by profit making motive or selfish interest. In India whole problem is arising due to devaluation of human values, Closely following the Vietnam War and the Watergate scandal, was a new awakening among the scholars of public administration manifested in the movement called New Public Administration which was conceptualized in the Minnowbrook Conference by young scholars at the leadership of Dwight Waldo. It emphasized the humanistic concerns in public administration and thus argued for delegation, social equity and similar social values.

Osborne and Gaebler's '*Re-inventing Government*' entered in the United States Government *via* Al Gore's Report on the *National Performance Review* (NPR) 1993. The NPR is the outcome of an in-depth six month study of the US Federal bureaucracy carried out by 250 public employees under the leadership of the then American Vice-President Al Gore. It must measure the performance of their agencies focusing on outcomes, not on inputs. The report of Al Gore's National Performance Review (1993) prefers the term 'democratic governance' to 'good governance' and its distinguishing attributes lie in certain 'values', such as justice, democracy etc.[22]

In 1997 Osborne, Gaebler and Peter Plastrik identified five strategies in connection with re-inventing Government—effectiveness, entrepreneurship, responsiveness, creativeness, and accountability. If we look into the Social Capital Theories of which Robert Putnam is associated as one of the leading advocates we find that it underlines the citizens' participation.[23]

The Government, prior to late 20th century was portrayed as the potent solution to all social problems. The emergence of concepts like 'Welfare State', 'Administrative State' has brought change to this view, especially since the later part of the last century the responsibility of the state has increased beyond expectation. The government of a democratic state has failed to render service to the people to their satisfaction. People have noticed that in most cases government itself cause problems. The inefficiency, lack of innovative capacity of the state machinery, rampant corruption in public services have become prominent. These widen the path of re-assertion on accountability, social equity, humanistic approach and similar other concerns in public administration leading to bold assertion on re-orientation of public administration towards public with humanistic view. Thus there emerged the concept of good governance.

Concept and Nature of Good Governance: According to UN Economic and Social Commission for Asia and Pacific (UNESPACP) Good Governance has eight characteristics: (1) Participation; (2) Rule of Law; (3) Transparency; (4) Responsiveness; (5) Consensus oriented; (6) Equity and Inclusiveness; (7) Effectiveness and Efficiency; and (8) Accountability.

A Global Forum to address Government for re-invention was first organized by the Government of United States in 1999. Since then it has emerged as one of the most significant global events to address the issue. Subsequent Forums have been organized by the Governments of Brazil, Italy, Morocco, Mexico met regularly. The seventh meeting of the Global Forum was held in UN at the instance of the Under Secretary General of it. It also highlighted several features of good governance, such as effectiveness, efficiency, accountability etc.[24]

United Nations of Organization also played a significant role in constructing and mapping the province of good governance. For renovating existing governance to achieve the standard of good governance reform of three areas is required-the state, the private sector and civil society. UN, while suggesting reform of existing governance across the world explicitly stated that the multi-colour culture of the global society need not be destroyed and it also adopted a liberal view towards the process of reform. The movement for reform in each nation may build good governance based on their own culture, own need hierarchy system to make the movement effective. However, there are certain common fundamental ingredients of good governance. These are– participation, rule of law, consensus oriented, equity and inclusiveness, effectiveness and efficiency, accountability, transparency and responsiveness.[25]

Participation: Participation in the administration and the political system of a country by both men and women is the key cornerstone of good governance. In different capacities people participate in democracy – as citizen, as taxpayer, as client or as service receiver, as member of the society and so on. Participation may be direct or indirect. The members of the Government including the administrators are directly involved in the administration of a country in the sense that they are policy formulators and implementers for the good and progress of the country. The other professionals, like physicians, teachers, lawyers, social workers, religious leaders, different associations or organizations can contribute through advices, expression of views and other related activities as the situation demands and thus play a significant in the administration of a democratic country.

Rule of Law: Good governance requires fair legal frameworks that are enforced impartially. It also requires protection of human rights. Just as impartial enforcement of laws requires independent and impartial police force and bureaucracy, for satisfactory medical services there is the need of skilled physicians with human qualities. The Rule of Law is one of the basic principles of democracy. The Rule of Law (also known as Nomocracy) is the legal principle that law should govern a nation, as opposed to arbitrary decisions by individual government officials. It may primarily refer to the influence and authority of law within a society, particularly as a constraint upon behaviour, including the behaviour of government officials. The phrase can be traced back to 16th century England and it was popularized in the Nineteenth century by British jurist A.V. Dicey. The concept was familiar to ancient philosophers such as Aristotle, to whom law should govern.

Rule of Law implies that every citizen is subject to law, including law makers themselves. In this sense, it stands in contrast to an autocracy, collective leadership, dictatorship or oligarchy where the rulers are above the law. Lack of the rule of law generally figures in dictatorships. It also occurs due to ignorance of the law and worst consequences of non-adherence of law, corruption, or lack of corrective mechanisms for administrative abuse.

A Secretary General of United Nations defined Rule of Law as a principle of governance in which all persons, institutions and entities, private and public, including the state itself, are accountable to laws that are publicly promulgated, equally enforced and independently adjudicated, and which are consistent with international human rights norms and standards. It requires, as well measures to ensure adherence to the principles of supremacy of laws, equality before law, accountability to the law, fairness in the applicability of law, separation of powers, participation in decision making, legal certainty, avoidance of arbitrariness and procedural and legal transparency.[26]

In the language of Justice V.R. Krishna Iyer the rule of law to be worthy must rise to a higher consciousness, so that every man must be able to manifest his capabilities despite his disabilities, through a dynamic discovery of himself, assisted in the process by the society in the field of education, employment, cultural exercises and the pursuit of happiness. When a person is sub-normal or abnormal, deformed or deprived in some function or faculty he is not viewed with hostility as a menace or a nuisance but a retardate in need of rehabilitation, an afflicted individual who can contribute to community development, given propitious circumstances. These possibilities, however, assume that the disabled individual has access to systems and services and legal rights assuring such access. Basically, disabled citizens have the same needs as others in the general population and when their potential is realized they contribute to the society. When they are cheered through arts and sports a new joy spreads. Likewise, when their faculties are not fertilized, there is social wastage.

The Constitution of India reflects the nation's value system and its mission. The Preamble to the constitution itself underlines 'justice, social, economic and ...; equality of status and opportunity;...and...the dignity of the individual.' The generosity of the concept of social justice assures to every member of the society fair treatment. This is for what Gandhi fought for during his life time. The framers of the constitution did not forget their obligation to it. [27]

Consensus Orientation: There are several actors in the process of governing a state. Good governance requires to reach a broad consensus in a society on what is in the best interest of community and how this can be achieved. It also requires a broad and long-term perspective on what is needed for sustainable human development and to achieve the goals of such development. This is possible from an understanding of the historical, cultural and social contexts of a given society.

Equity and Inclusiveness: A society's well-being depends on ensuring that all its members feel that they have a say in it and do not feel excluded from the mainstream of the society. It requires all groups, but particularly the most vulnerable, have opportunities to improve and maintain well-being. There are several actors in the process of governing a state. Good governance requires to reach a broad consensus in a society on what is in the best interest of community and how this can be achieved.

Effectiveness and Efficiency: Good governance means the processes and institutions which produce result that meet the needs of the society while making the best use of resources at their disposal. The concept of good governance also covers the sustainable use of natural resources and the protection of the environment.

Accountability: Accountability is a key requirement of good governance. Not only the government institutions, but the private and civil society organizations must be accountable to the public and to their institutional stakeholders. O.G. Stahl is very close to Gandhi in solving human problems when he said that the constructive ways to develop a sense of responsibility or accountability to a great extent on the calibre of the management that recruits candidates on merit and supervision that develops ways to motivate personnel to be committed to the goal of the service. The positive connotation of accountability reminds us that India needs durably competent, ethical and accountable civil servants. The most suitable way to achieve it is through serious attention to the best precepts of personnel management rather than through disparagement of public employment and absurd, unworkable prohibitions or punitive measures. However, he did not rule out the need of negative restraints.

Public accountability is a matter of attitude of public servants towards public. P.R. Dubhasi pointed out that public administration should be efficient but it is more important that it should be ethical. Accountability is not just in the negative sense of holding public servants responsible for their lapses. It has a positive connotation. They have the responsibility to discharge duties which are of great public significance.[28]

Accountability is an essential part of every act of a man, especially when he or she does it in public capacity or as service provider to the people. A public servant is a trustee of public fund, a major part of which is constituted by the taxes paid by the citizens.

The citizens may also be called as taxpayers. Every act of a public servant has not only financial implication but also moral implication. A public servant exercises the authority entrusted to the position of which he or she is an incumbent. However, the incumbent must exercise the authority in the interest of the taxpayers. Even the salary may be said as compensation, as it is paid for the services rendered by a public servant to the people. Therefore, the public servants must be accountable or answerable for their activities to the public. In a modern democracy various devices are adopted to ensure accountability of the public servants. But, the sense of accountability must be rooted in the heart of a person to make the external devices effective. Significantly, it is cultivated at the family and is gradually strengthened in the environment created by educational institutions and later in the service career of an individual.

In a modern democracy accountability is a strong device to secure people's active cooperation for the success of administration to serve the human society. People are familiar and more concern with the financial accountability only. We are yet to underline ethical accountability in the public service, though it constitutes a significant part of democratic administration. We must give a serious thought to the issue that the main root cause of financial irregularities is ethical vacuity.

Accountability helps maintaining efficiency, reducing errors, strengthening social relationship amongst the persons within an organization and also between an organization and public and enhancing the reputation of the organization. A reputed organization itself is a strong motivating factor to make its members work hard and to command confidence of the client.[29]

Transparency: It means that information is freely available and directly accessible to those who are affected by such decisions and their enforcement. It also means that enough information are provided through media in easily understandable forms so that people are benefited. This is the fundamental requirement in almost all the services, especially in the medical services for mainly three reasons—(1) Skilled of the physician is his own monopoly, which the patients and attendants cannot acquire; (2) Patient has immense faith on the doctor; and (3) The attendants suffer from acute anxiety and always want early recovery of the patient. Just as the conflict between police and public arises very frequently as the police meet people mostly in the controversial situations. Similarly, doctors always meet people who are vulnerable due to illness accompanied by the tension ridden attendants. The rules and regulations of the Police Department must be transparent and easily understandable to all kinds of people to avoid conflict and also to maintain discipline in the society. Similarly, the transparency and easily understandable communication of the status of the patient and the nature of the treatment may reduce anxiety of the attendants which may help disappearance of conflicting responsiveness: Good governance requires that institutions and processes try to serve all stakeholders within a reasonable timeframe.[30]

Public Opinion: In good governance the public opinion is very important in the sense that through it the citizens exercise their sovereign power, i.e. the sovereignty of the people. The phrase 'public opinion' in the sense of "popular participation in the creation, control, execution and criticism of public policy" was first used in France and was found in the writings of Rousseau. The phrase came into prominence because of its association with democracy. The people must ensure governmental accountability and responsiveness. They must, through public opinion, control the power holders and ensure that their common good is realized. Public opinion is also viewed as a kind consensus among people which emerges in major issues of governmental policies and administration. This view carried with it the assumption that the public was interested in public policy, that people thought and acted rationally, that they voted intelligently and that the view of the majority was enacted into law. Further, it was believed that an alert and vigilant public would ensure that public policy was based on the principles of social justice and morality. In spite of various controversies on the concept, formation of opinions and several other emerging constraints in the contemporary world pubic opinion's significance in democracy is not diminishing.[31]

Communication: Communication is another very important element of good governance. It is a process, and information is the 'thing' that is communicated, as said by Mohit Bhattacharya. The word 'communication' is derived from Latin word *communis* which means 'common'. In a communication process, the sender of information seeks to establish a commonness with the receiver of information. Therefore, communication may be defined as the use of words, letters, symbols or some other means to have common information about the object of interest.[32]

Herbert Alexander Simon defined communication as a flow of information downwards, upwards and sideways in an organization. It is essential for effective functioning of an organization. However, the nature of information and advice to be tendered may change from situation to situation. Therefore, collecting dependable information and proper utilization of it ensures greater effectiveness in the decision-making and provides adequate line of communication and persuasion.[33]

In the system of communication there is the possibility of being influenced by Helmsman, said Norbert Weiner. Being influenced by Hobbesian thought Weiner believed in the natural tendency towards disorder and disintegration in society. This has to be fought back by methodical information processing which is the hallmark of organization. Weiner's theme is that man can control and modify his environment only through information, and this information is transmitted *via*-messages. The flow and feedback of information has a significant effect on human behaviour. The most widely used model has evolved from the work of Shannon and Weaver, and Schramm according to which the basic ingredients of the model include a source, an encoder, a message channels, a decoder and a purpose for communicating.

The source is usually a member with ideas, conformation and a purpose for communicating. The function of encoding is to provide a form in which ideas and purposes can be expressed as a message for transmittal. The message is the actual physical product that is conveyed. The channels stand for carriers of messages from the source to the receiver, including written, telephonic and numerous other models. The must be decoded in terms of relevance to the receiver. Then feedback from the receiver's end "Communicate" is a very old word. It has had many meanings in the course of its history. Daniel J. Boorstin in his book, "*Democracy and Its Discontents*" pointed out in this context Starkey's *History of England* in 1538 where Thomas Starkey, the English Political Theorist and Humanist said the word "communicate" is a part of the definition of God. To him God is He who "communicated" His goodness to all others. This, however, is related to the word "Communicant," a person who shares in the Eucharist. In origin, "communicate" is related to the word "Common" or "Community" and it means somehow to make common or share.

Boorstin accordingly defined the rise of civilization as the rise of communication – the improvement of the ways of sharing and the improvement of that which is shared. It is obvious that the quality of any civilization will depend on what is there to share and on how it is shared. Any democracy, more than any other form of government, is based on the faith that sharing the good things of life – and especially sharing the power to govern—can be wholesome.

While the progress of civilization is an improvement in what we share and in the processes of sharing, there is another commonly forgotten essential to the rise of civilization which has been pointed out by Sigmund Freud. To him an indispensable feature of civilization is the willingness of people not to say and not to do many things that might want to say or do. This is one way of describing a decent society and in its most everyday form a way of describing good manners.[34]

The formal communication system in the administrative hierarchy as analyzed by Max Weber may become dysfunctional. Under this system communication has to flow upward and downward through proper channel. But in practice communication flows almost entirely downward and are often distorted at the middle levels during the process. Those who are at the top of the hierarchy are to be aware of the problems or feelings of those at the bottom. Because the structure of a bureaucracy is essentially authoritarian, officials at the lower levels may conceal defects, mistakes and inefficiencies from their superiors. Here the need arises to assert on the normative aspects of governance, i.e. good governance.[35]

Social Relationship: Every organization, in ultimate analysis, is a social organization. The individuals working in it develop social relations among themselves. Douglas McGregor pointed out that behind every managerial decision or action are assumptions about human nature and human behaviour.[36] There is no easy way to improve employee relations. Basically, the problem is moral and ethical.[37] The informal organization, i.e. social relationship is an inalienable part of formal organization and it produces two kinds of influence on formal organization. It establishes certain norms, attitudes, understandings, habit etc. and *secondly*, it creates an environment in which the formal organization has to function. Social norms and customs are very powerful with wide coverage of personnel system for smooth functioning of a formal organization. The environment created by social relationship is a precondition for accepting or rejecting common strategies, determination of means of communication. This human aspect of organization was highlighted by the Hawthorne Study made by a group of researchers under the leadership of George Elton Mayo (1880-1949).

Hawthorne experiment has showed that an organization is a social system with group relationship and group attitudes. It reflects the informal aspect of an organization. An organization is a complex system as it depends for its success on interdependence of individuals, their motives, attitudes, behaviour etc. Besides formal rules and regulations informal relationship is an inalienable part of an organization. It generally originates in continuous interactions, contacts and relationships which are not at all a part of formal system. These contacts may be incidental or accidental to organized activities or may arise from personal desire or gregarious instincts.

These informal relations are necessary to the operation of formal organizations as a means of communication, cohesion and protecting the personality and integrity of the individual. This informal relationship serves certain objectives—(a) helps attainment of personal objectives; (b) provides social satisfaction; (c) makes communication easy; and (d) ensure social control of behaviour.

It is true that formal organization cannot be replaced by informal organization. But it fills the gaps in an organization and helps effective functioning of it. S.R. Maheswari, in his book titled, '*Administrative Theory*' emphasized the need of informal organization to meet the deficiencies of rules or policies. These rules generally lack dynamism unless interpreted by the personnel working in the organization to ensure effective implementation with the human spirit of the laws or policies.[38]

Moral Leadership: Moral leadership is one which is directed by respect for ethical beliefs and human value and human dignity.

A moral leader must be a man of reason and capacity, skill and curiosity for knowledge and his main aim is to serve the people selflessly.

It is the responsibility of a leader to take care of morale in an organization. In a broad sense morale, group spirit, state of mind etc. express themselves in loyalty, enthusiasm, cooperation, pride in the service, and devotion to duty of the personnel working in an organization. Morale is defined as the capacity of a group of people to pull together persistently and consistently in pursuit of a common purpose. It depends on (i) the confidence of the individual members in the purpose of the group; (ii) the confidence they have in the leadership; (iii) the confidence they have in each other; the organizational efficiency of the group, both formally and informally; and (iv) mental, emotional and physical health of the individual.[39]

Democracy and Human Rights: The word "Democracy" has become a common word used by the citizens of a modern state. They have enough faith in the democratic principles. But experience in India shows that in reality average people do not practice them in their lives though they have faith in them and express the need of these principles in public speeches and writings. Adherence of democratic principles or to follow a democratic way of life is not an easy task. It requires perseverance, mental strength and commitment to the cause of humanity. It is also a difficult task as the whole concept of democracy centres round human being and success of democracy depends on activism of human power along with other qualities.

The concept of democracy cannot be understood fully without reference to human rights. The journey of a man from the status of cave-man who was exposed to all kinds of natural calamities and attacks of wild animals to that of democratic man, who is safeguarded on every aspect of his life was piloted by faith in human rights and dignity. During this period man had to struggle against the violent forces of nature and wild animals in every walk of life. This journey will always remind us that human rights are not created in thin air. These are the results of untiring and long struggle of man for survival. In course of journey man has realized the dignity of human being. And explicit expression of it is found in the emergence of the concept of democracy.[40]

The responsibility for deterioration democratic governance must be shared by both the rulers and the ruled. While discussing this issue we have to underline the state as the largest component of the governance, which belongs, along with others, to the socially, economically and educationally backward classes also and to those who are exploited by political leaders, money lenders, social workers, administrators, private businessmen etc. The emergence of large number of false educational institutions at higher levels and false financial organizations are appearing as a serious threat to humanity, the key to democracy. The Leading personalities in the fields of politics, administration, education, social work, religions constitute very significant component of the Indian governance. They are the role models for the rest of the society. Unfortunately, experience shows that most of them maintain multi standards of life which is not easily understandable by the common men. They hide their inner motive very skilfully while approaching the general masses for participation in their programmes. They have become slaves of money and move as directed by money power. Naturally, they lose the capacity to judge what is good and what is bad even for their own lives. Criminalization of politics is a serious ailment in Indian democracy affecting the human rights of the people at every walk of life. The administration is not responsive, responsible and accountable to the public for their activities. The common people are exploited and cheated by falsehood and dishonesty in various forms. As mentioned above it is not because of lack of laws or rules and regulations and institutions to safeguard human rights of different sections of the people. What is lacking is the obedience to human values and human dignity. Today priority is given to accumulation of money by any means and any amount without limitation and building of huge property—movable or immovable at the cost of human rights of our own people. Now the question before us is how to save the human beings from this new form of slavery caused by the money and muscle power in modern India. Disraeli said, "Money is not the measure of a man, but it is often the means of finding out how small he is." It is difficult no doubt but not impossible to redirect the society towards humanity so that each individual can be released from uncomfortable stay in the domain of monetary slavery.

The concept 'Good Governance' has ethical or normative connotation, which helps to judge 'good' and 'bad' governance indicating certain features of it. The definition of 'Good

Governance' formulated by the World Bank incorporates this feature. It defined "Good Governance" as 'the one epitomized by predictable, open, an enlightened policy-making, a bureaucracy imbued with a professional ethos acting in furtherance of the public good, the rule of law, transparent processes, and a strong civil society participating in public affairs. Poor governance, on the other hand, is characterized arbitrary policy-making, unaccountable bureaucracies, enforced by unjust legal systems, the abuse of executive power, and wide spread corruption."[41]

While referring to the responsibility of the people it may be mentioned that the basic ideals of democracy or self-rule is not new to the Indian tradition. The Indian history, culture and philosophy tell us that the kingship and monarchy were the outcome of people's democratic thoughts. Though the king was the supreme ruler, the will of the people was reflected in the administration. Another positive aspect of Indian democracy is that the democratic values were flooded in the ancient heritage of India. Even though the king and the institution of kingship were hereditary, the king had to administer with the advice and cooperation of the assembly and committee of the councillors.[42]

What is needed today is that we, the modern Indians, have to visit our past to X-ray those values in the perspective of good governance. The other reasons for calling good governance as democratic governance are based on the commonality of keys in both types of administration.

Today public administration is close not merely to politics but also to private administration. The concept of e-governance widens the scope for thinking of inclusiveness nature of public administration, and facilitates implementation of global policies like 'Health for All', 'Sports for All', 'Education for All' etc. by the nation-states asserting the need of inclusiveness nature of public administration. It strengthens democratic administration which is the basis of good governance.[43]

However, in recent years the scientific approach is adopted to study both the administrative and social problems to take effective decisions for their solution. But one cannot claim to have knowledge on the exactness of the problems of the people. The simple reason is that the administrators deal with human beings who are independent organisms by themselves, who have the thinking capacity, who are conscious, who are also expert in hiding their true nature when they choose to do. They cannot be made subject of experiment or study on scientific basis.

What is needed today is that the public servants must be active in the policy process being involved in scientific analysis, correct diagnosis of the problems and aspiration of the people and understanding of the political implication of the policy. Further they must be highly sensitive to the notion of public interest and moral context their action. Today the administration is de-emphasizing the public aspect of public administration and thereby destroying the democratic values of administration.

Here mention may be made of the concept of professionalism. *The Merriam-Webster Dictionary defines* "professionalism" as the conduct, aims or qualities that characterize or mark a profession or a professional person," and it defines profession as "a calling requiring specialized knowledge and often long and intensive academic preparation." This definition of professionalism encompasses a number of different attributes. These are:

Specialized Knowledge: The professionals are known for their specialized knowledge and deep commitment to develop and improve their skills. They have to work in a serious, thoughtful and sustained way to acquire knowledge needed for successful performance in the field. They must keep the knowledge up-to-date so that they can continue to deliver the best work possible.

Competence: professionals always focus on finding solutions, do not make any excuse.

Honesty and Integrity: Honesty and integrity are two significant qualities of the professionals by which they can secure confidence of the people. They never compromise their values. More than this, true professionals are humble – if a project or job falls outside their scope of expertise, they have the courage to admit this. They are always willing to learn from the competent persons.

Accountability: Professionals hold themselves accountable for their thoughts, words and actions, especially when they make any mistake. This personal accountability is closely tied up with honesty and integrity.

Self-Regulation: Professionals have self-regulation while dealing with the people.

Image: Professionals always try to maintain impressive image of the institution in which they work on the people whom they are to serve.

Emotional Intelligence: Professionals must be polite and demonstrate humane behaviour to others. They must listen patiently while receiving complaints from others. They always take care of advance planning, time management and planning skill.[44]

The global community ultimately requires the emergence of a responsive moral society, avoiding the use of force and coercion in national and international disputes. Values and norms that are not codified into laws, and laws that lack enforcement mechanisms, will have no tangible effect. Thus globalization is intertwined with the articulation of new collective rights and ethics, and the ensuing impact on national and international norms and institutions.[45]

REFERENCES

1. Dubhasi, P.R. (2016). *Administrative Reforms*, B.R. Publishing Corporation, Delhi.
2. En.wikipedia.org/Moral_responsibility: accessed on 17.6.2014.
3. Kapur, A.C. (2003). *Principles of Political Science*, Published by S. Chand & Company, New Delhi.
4. http://en.wikipedia.org/wiki/philosophy, 19.4.2018.
5. Kennedy, John, F. (1956). *Profiles in Courrage*. Text compilation by Ombica Gupta, Art by Kanti Roy; published by William D. Miller for the United States Information Service, Sikandra Road, New Delhi.
6. Buggi, "Chandra Sekhar: Relevance of Gandhian Political Ideas Today." *Journal of Gandhian Studies*, Volume 5. No. 18, January 1978 published by Institute of Gandhian Thought and Peace Studies, Gandhi Bhawan, University of Allahabad.
7. Rao, V. Venkata (1980). *History of Political Theories*; S. Chand & Company, New Delhi.
8. Rohr, John A.: Ethics in Public Administration: a State-of-the-Discipline Report: edited by Naomi B. Lynn and Aaron Wildavsky, East-West Electric Press Pvt. Limited, New Delhi.
9. Dennis F. Thompson (1983) article "Bureaucracy and Democracy" in the book *Democratic Theory and Practice*, ed. By G. Duncan, Cambridge University Press, referred by Robert B. Denhardt: art. Public Administration Theory: the State of the Discipline: published in the book titled, *Public Administration (State of the Discipline)* edited by Naomi B. Lynn and Aaron Wildavsky, East-West Electric Press Pvt. Limited New Delhi, 1990.
10. Jain, R.B. (2013). Art. "Reinventing Good Governance: Challenges and Strategies in India; in the book titled, *Governance and Society*; edited by Neelam Trivedi and others, Rawat Publications, New Delhi.

11. Bhelkey, S.E. (2002). Art. "Inadequacy of Democracy," in the book, *Governance and Human Rights*, edited by Bharat Jhunjhunwala; Kalpaz Publications, New Delhi.
12. Haldipur, R.N. "The Citizen, Society and Decision-making, in *IJPA*; Spl. issue on Citizen-Administration-I July–September Vol. XXI No. 3.
13. Chapter 2, "Democratic Governance for Human Development;" in Human Development Report 2002, published for the United Nations Development Programme (UNDP), New York, Oxford; Oxford University Press 2002.
14. United Nations –Public Administration in the Second United Nations Development Decade: report of the Second Meeting of Experts (ST/TAO/M/57), 1971.
15. United Nations –Decentralization for National and Local Development Decade: report of the Second Meeting of Experts (ST/TAO/M/19), 1971).
16. Chapter 2, "Democratic Governance for Human Development;" in Human Development Report 2002, published for the United Nations Development Programme (UNDP), New York, Oxford; Oxford University Press 2002.
17. Iyer, V.R. Krishna (1980). *Justice and Beyond*, Deep and Deep Publications; New Delhi.
18. economics.about.com/globalizationtrade/aaglobalization.htm
19. www.fibre2fashion.com/industry-article/8738/ompact-of-globalization1.asp
20. UN, (2001). *World Public Sector Report: Globalization and the State*, New Work.
21. economics.about.com/globalizationtrade/aaglobalization.htm
22. Maheswari, S.R. (2002). *Administrative Theory*; 2nd edition; Macmillan India Ltd. Delhi.
23. www.mildredwarner-org/govt-restructuring/re-inventing-govt.www.unpan.org/DPADM/Events/GlobalForumReinventing government/tabid/441/language/en-US/default.aspx
24. www.mildredwarner-org/govt-restructuring/re-inventing-govt.
25. https://en.wikipedia.or/wiki/Good_governance 25.1.2018.
26. http://en.wikipedia.org/wiki/Rule_of_law 6.12.2014.
27. V.R. Krishna Iyer (1980). *Justice and beyond*: Deep and Deep Publications; Rajouri Garden, New Delhi.
28. Dubhasi, P.R.: *Ibid.*
29. En.wikipedia.org/Moral_responsibility: accessed on 17.6.2014.
30. www.unescap.org/pdd/prs/ProjectActivities/Ongoing/gg/governance/.asp
31. Valsangkar, Krishna, Marina Pinto, Louis D'Silva (1980). *Aspects of Political Theory*; Orient Longman; Kolkata.
32. Bhattacharya, Mohit (1987). *Public Administration*, The World Press Private Ltd., Kolkata.

33. Ravindra Prasad, V.S. Prasad, P. Satyanarayana and Y. Pardhasaradhi (2011). *Administrative Thinkers*, Sterling Publishers, New Delhi.
34. Boorstin, Daniel J. (1974). *Democracy and Its Discontents:* Random House, New York.
35. Robertson, Ian (1980). *Sociology*; Worth Publishing, inc.
36. McGregor (1960), *The Human Side of Enterprise*, McGraw-Hill New York.
37. James C. Worthy and James, C. (1959). *Big Business and Free Men*, Harper New York.
38. Maheswari: 2002, *Ibid.*
39. Stahl, O.G. (1962). *Public Personnel Administration*, fifth edition, Oxford & IBH Publishing Co., New Delhi.
40. Palkhiwala, Nani (1997). We, The People; UBS Publisher and Distributors Ltd., Delhi.
41. R.B. Jain: *Ibid.*
42. Bhelkey, S.E. (2002). "Inadequacy of Democracy", in *Governance and Human Rights*, edited by Bharat Jhunjhunwala, Kalpaz Publications.
43. Denhardt, Robert, B. (1990). "Public Administration Theory: The State of the Discipline; in *Public Administration (State of the Discipline)* edited by Naomi B. Lynn and Aaron Wildavsky, East-West Electric Press Pvt. Limited, New Delhi.
44. https://www.linkedin.com/pulse/what-professionalism-does-mean-you-daniel-w-porcupile, 4.8.2018.
45. Khatami, Seyed Mohmmad, President of the Islamic Republic of Iran: (2002) Human Development Report 2002, published for the United Nations development Programme (UNDP), Oxford University Press, New York, Oxford.

V
Ethical Response to Corruption

To eradicate corruption in the modern world various laws, rules and regulations, provisions for punishments are provided at both national and international levels. In addition to judicial system, grievance redressal machineries are also established in the pattern of Scandinavian Ombudsman in different countries including India. New departments are created, structural changes are made in the existing administrative systems of the nation states with a view to reduce corruption in democracy. But day by day corruption is increasing at every walk of life in the contemporary world. It has become the global concern to save the world from the scourge of this problem.

The source of corruption in administration as well as in the society is basically the man's way of life which is controlled by his thought process. Therefore, to eradicate corruption democratic principles or ethical guidelines may be considered as the suitable supplementary measure to fill the gap of existing efforts of the nations for reducing corruption. United Nations Organization also organized international conventions to find out solution to this serious global problem. These efforts of the UN reflect the need of re-assertion of human values and ethical principles. Edward Gamaya Hoseah said, "Good Governance Architacture" is meant to provide a working solution to curb unethical behaviour, corruption, and the culture of impunity." This working solution involves economic and institutional reforms, prevention strategies, enforcement, political will, transparency, accountability, popular participation, rule of law and the democratic space. Good governance is not a theoretical design; rather, it is a practical tool that can overcome corruption and associated malpractices that thwart development and the values and growth of democratic institutions.[1]

I have already indicated in the previous chapter that good governace has a normative connotation and it can change the way of man's life and can work as a strong weapon to rehumanize the contemporary global society and re-invent modern democracy.

Ethical response is an effective device to eradicate corruption in administration or in any social organization. Ethics generates human power which is essential to fight against corruption in any field of the man's life. Because, corruption is a human problem. Therefore, ultimate solution of this problem is human power. Laws, rules and regulations, codes etc. can create an environment in which the road to human power becomes clear to be active.

Man's psychology consists of mainly three elements – rational faculty, passion and habit. To acquire virtues and to sustain them he has to habitualize these virtues. Since man is a social animal he must go through the process of socialization to develop good habits so that he can move through rational self-direction. He has irrational elements also. Kantilal Das in his article, "Why Environmental Ethics Matter to Philosophy?" refers what Greek philosopher Aristotle said, man is the rational animal. Indian philosophy also tells us the way in which spiritual and moral unity can be awakened in man to realize his own self. It also helps to humanize a man. The writings of Mahatma Gandhi, Rabindranath Tagore, Swami Vivekananda and several other Indian thinkers unfolded the ways to be adopted for humanization of our society and to prevent the process of dehumanization. Referring to the contribution of development of science and technology, one cannot deny its contribution to the human civilization. At the same time the misuse of science and technology causes several environmental and social problems in the modern time such as, Ozone depletion, water pollution, global warming, various kinds of ailments etc. It is noticed that the exposure to the facilities provided by modern science and technology sharpens the greediness of individuals. Gradually, man has climbed down from 'man of need' to 'man of greed'. The negative impact of it is very harmful to the human society. A man of greed does not know the limit of the man's requirements, just as a suspicious man does not know where the end of suspicion is. Referring to the negative impact on the health of a man one may point out that it makes a man more lazy by providing all kinds of comfort in life making him unable to undertake even the minimum physical activities required for health due to which Government has to make provision for 'walking zones' in cities for maintining heath of the people. The harmful impact of science and technology is also reflected in agro-based eatable items. Misuse of information technology causes distortion of social fabrics, especially in the field of parental and social control over the youth of a country. It may be considered that the achievement of science is purely materialistic and they are not unqualifiedly good in themselves.[3]

Since good governance is nothing but democratic governance let us have a look into it. Democracy is the well accepted system of government across the world. Since the time of ancient Athenian democracy it is occupying a unique position in the political world of a state without giving any scope to think of replacing it by an alternative system of government, excepting making it indirect in nature for administrative convenience. The indirect democracy is also called representative democracy because under this system people control the government through elected officials.

In course of time, ostensibly democratic organizations or institutions fall short of fulfilling the democratic principles in their practices. It results the appearance of democratic deficit (democracy deficit) like a giant distorting the fundamental principles of democracy. The concept of democracy is reduced to that of election system only, not beyond it. And to maintain its representative nature the leaders use to pick up members according to their choice from different communities. They do not care to realize the implication of the term 'representative'. Cash for Vote, Cash for Job, Emotional Exploitation of Voters etc. have become tools of electoral system. These are the indicators of recent trends of political participation in modern democracy.

The unwelcome trends in political democracy around the world encouraged member states to pronounce on the floor of UNO the Millenium Declaration as, "We will spare no effort to promote democracy and strengthen the rule of law, as well as respect for all internationally recognized human rights and fundamental freedom." At the UN General Assembly in 2000, heads of state and government took stock of gross inequalities in human development worldwide and recognized "their collective responsibility to uphold the principles of human dignity, equality and equity at the global level."

Now in the Twenty first century the primary task of us is to make a collective effort to put an end of the process of dehumanization of democracy across the world. For this nobody can deny the need of reduction of corruption in the global human village by reasserting the moral dimension of governance.[4]

Democracy cannot be imposed nor it can be imported from abroad. It is a way of life of the individuals equipped with human qualities. The seeds of democracy are sown in the family in which the child is born. It is the mother who helps the child to internalize the democratic ideals through behaviour and habitualization of democratic way of life. Then educational institutions deepen these habits in their lives through formal education.

The process of habitualization is a part of the process of socialization to make a man from being to becoming. This process begins at the stage of leaning by a child—'how to walk', 'how to talk', 'how to address others' etc. At this stage of the life journey immediately after his birth provision is made for human infrastructure consisting of love, affection, attention, care and appreciation by mother and other members of the family. It is a two way process in the sense that the child responses to them in his own way of expression during that period. Gradually, he can reciprocate to it explicitly in his own words and behaviour. Human environment is intact till he goes to school. In school he is exposed to a new environment in which the human environment, in which much attention is paid to the learning of preliminaries of education. Naturally, he may notice some changes in the infrastructure and environment. There may be conflict in his mind. Here problem arises to sustain human infrastructure and environment for him. Gradually the problem becomes very complicated. In this juncture it is the responsibility of the educational institutions to make every attempt to help the child to carry out the human qualities in his journey of education. Must care has to be taken to develop his good habits and to sustain the habits through practice. What he earns by way of habitualization is reflected in his behaviour during service life. He goes on confirming his behavioural values and adding new values, reforming his old behaviours through action and interaction with his fellow workers and superiors.

The notable point is that though man has the capacity to

rationalize his behaviour and acquire human qualities, the irrational elements exist in his or inner personality. If environment is polluted with various kinds of social diseases he may be affected by them very easily to sharpen his irrational elements. Man is by nature lazy and whenever he gets the opportunity of avoiding difficult work he avoids it. For example, to maintain a disciplined life one has to work hard, whenever he gets the opportunity to avoid it he does it. Further man is the seeker of comfort. Experience shows that more we are in the process of modernization more we are becoming seeker of comfort even at the heavy cost of the family and the nation. Therefore, care has to be taken to deactivate the element of passion in man at every stage of his life by creating ethical environment.

All institutions, both formal and informal including family are practical as well as normative in character. They can create environment for development of moral or ethical behaviour of individuals which influences people both within and outside the institutions. In democratic country the members of these institutions play a very significant role in making the governance effective. The ethical issues in public service organizations are a mixture of individual motivation, organizational imperative and social values. These cannot be achieved in an institution which consists of corrupt personnel. Therefore, the ethical issues have to be taken care of in every public institution to eradicate corruption along with other requirements.[5]

The word "Ethics" is defined by the *Concise Oxford Dictionary* as "the science of morals." The utility of ethics rests on the fact that it helps a decision-maker to search for morally acceptable decision. Chester Barnard has described moral behaviour as behaviour, "governed by beliefs or feelings of what is right or wrong regardless of self-interest or immediate consequences of a decision to do or not to do specific things under particular conditions."[6]

Ethics is the study of morality. Morality is the value dimension of human decision-making and behaviour. The language of morality includes nouns such as, 'rights', 'responsibilities' and 'virtue' and adjective such as, 'good' and 'bad', 'right' and wrong', 'just' and 'unjust'. According to these concepts ethics is primarily a matter of knowing or it has theoretical perspective where as morality is a matter of doing, it has practical perspective. Ethics provides the rational criteria on the basis of which people can decide or behave. Ethics embraces almost all the aspects of human behaviour. Ethical principles represent moral values or standards governing the conduct of an individual. Ethics is a Greek word. It means moral character. Again morality is a Latin word indicating custom or manner. Ethics and morality are two sides of the same coin—one is the theory of right action and the other is its practice. Ethics is a study of moral conduct.[7]

It is found that the subject of ethics deals with 'right' and 'wrong', 'should' or 'should not' rather than 'legal' and 'illegal'. It cannot be denied that the discussion on 'legal' and 'illegal' is grounded on ethical principles and human values. The ethical principles provide guidance to the organizational activism towards the predetermined goals. However, the ethical principles are not free from ambiguity as the nature and meaning of ethics vary with the variation of context, individuals and communities.[8]

Ethics is a strong human force to eradicate almost all kinds of problems in any social organization in the world. It is the most effective way to fight against the very destructive ailment like corruption in the governance as well as in the society. The simple reason is that the ethical principles centre round human being and similar is the position with that of corruption. It is the man who can act morally as well as immorally not the material or the system. Therefore, it is the man who can eradicate corruption in any organization. For this he has to be equipped with human qualities to build up ethical infrastructure in the organization. The laws of a country, the systems, rules and regulations can only create an environment for the growth of ethical or human infrastructure. The human infrastructure consists of love, affection, attention, appreciation and care of human being. A man begins his life in the midst of these elements after his birth. These are very well nurtured in the family at the leadership of his mother. When he comes to the school he is exposed to the formal environment which is another socializing agency. The educational institutions must create and sustain ethical infrastructure within which a child can develop his personality in a right direction. The responsibility of the school is to acknowledge the human culture of the students in addition to their academic achievements. The next major socializing agency if the work place or organization where the individual gets the opportunity to demonstrate his habit and culture and also to confirm, modify and accept new human qualities from the fellow beings and superiors through social relationship and code of conduct.

Since man has the rational faculty he proceeds in his life journey with conscious and self-awareness effort. Here what is needed is the sustenance of good habits and qualities which he carries with him to the work place. Further sharing of good habits amongst fellow members and superiors through communication is also very important in the interest of human values. I have the strong faith on what R.K. Misra has said the exposure of a man to the human environment will certainly enable him to develop the habit of self-direction in his life journey to become an asset of the global human society. However, it has to be admitted that it is a difficult task, because unhealthy environment will create scope to slip away from the right direction, which is very easy and provides immediate pleasure and comfort.[9]

Coming to the political world which plays a significant role in governance of a country indirect democracy is the accepted and popular political system across the world. In the contemporary world the concept of democracy has been narrowed down to the system of election only. Political participants, especially political parties have failed to look beyond the orbit of election. In election 'number' and 'voter' plays a significant role in deciding the majority party as ruling party and to acknowledge its legitimacy. Here the problem is the simplification of the concept of 'number' and 'voter'. This simplified version of these two words has distorted the true concept of democracy. Any student of political science or philosophy who studies Pythagoreanism knows the philosophy behind the 'number' insisted by Pythagoerans. To them justice is a number. But, this is a square number, not merely a number. In a square number there is harmony, because it is composed of equal parts. The implication of this principle is that a state is just so long as the principle of equality is maintained. To him as regards harmony, the number is very important and fundamental to it. Where there is harmony there is justice. Justice is a number. This number is a square number. In a square number there is harmony, because it is composed of equal parts. The implication of this principle is that a state is just so long as the principle of equality is maintained.[10]

Similarly, in modern democracy, no doubt number is the key,

i.e. the number of voters. The voter is a human being having reasoning power, not simply a voter without reasoning power. For that in every democratic country certain conditions have been imposed on the right to vote. The basic condition is the age of the voter. It indicates the assertion on equality of voters, the reasoning capacity of the individuals, and freedom of expression. Again, here also the notable point is that the political leaders have failed to allow the voters to exercise their reasoning capacity to select their representatives to have self-rule in the true sense of the term. They are stressing votes from the people with the help of money and muscle power, emotional exploitation by suppressing the reasoning and human power of the voters. The political parties have forgotten their major role as political socializing agency in the modern democracy to educate the innocent and ignorant voters. The experience in the Indian democracy compels the enlighten voters to have this feeling.

We should not forget that democracy is a process not an end. It is a way of functioning by both individuals and institutions to an end. The end is protection and development of human civilization. Here the notable point is that democratic process may differ depending on the nature of services or institutions. The threat to democracy arises not merely from the degenerated electoral system, but also from intolerance, lack of respect for human rights and human dignity during post-election system also. In the Twenty first century utmost care has to be taken to make state institutions function democratically in the face of globalization, liberalization and privatization. The nation-states are still powerful force in promoting the nation. What is necessary is the adoption of human approach to eradicate dysfunctioning of political and administrative system in a democracy. Here one has to think of widening the scope of social control through, culture, religion, human rights and human dignity, truth etc.

Culture: Culture of a society is a very strong factor to induce a man to work or render service to the people within the ethical framework. When we talk about culture generally we have in our mind the narrow expression of it indicating art, literature, dances, songs etc. The phrases like, 'Cultural Function', 'Cultural Show' and 'Cultural Procession' are commonly used by us in our day-to-day life. But, the sociologists use the term culture in a wider perspective with the coverage of entire way of social life. To them culture consists of all the shared products of human society. These products are of two kinds, material and non-material. While material products consist of physical objects, non-material culture consists of languages, ideas, beliefs, rules, customs, myths, skills, family patterns. Both society and culture are mutually dependent on each other for their survival.

Culture is the creation of man. At the same time he is also influenced by culture of the society of which he is a member. The cave-man invented the ways to produce fire, to cultivate land, to be protected from wild animals etc. He has thus invented ways to survive in the world of nature. He is still exploring different ways to adjust in the changing situation. He makes his own social environment inventing and sharing the rules and patterns of behaviour that shape his life, and he uses his acquired knowledge to change the natural environment as well. His social life is based on the habit of sharing culture. The social audit, social monitoring and social control on the adoption of social norms and behaviour pattern compel the members of the traditional society to be within the framework of the social culture. While transforming the traditional society to modern one he should not distort the human culture of the society to which he belongs.

Man does not inherit culture through the mechanism of birth. He acquires it from the social environment and through participation in different social activities. Obedience to elderly members of the family and family to the social leadership is another way to adopt social culture in the traditional society. It is an external force to regulate man's behaviour and discipline in the society. Robertson also stated that the contents of culture cannot be genetically transmitted. There is no gene that tells us to dance, to believe in a particular God, to build houses etc. Culture is thus a substitute for 'instinct' as a means of responding to the environment. Celebration of certain festivals, adherence to customs and traditions, maintenance of social relationship in a guided manner are the ideals or norms accepted by the society.

The codes are nothing but norms to ensure that social life is peaceful and secured. For they give us guidelines within the framework of which individuals have to behave and these codes help establishment and promotion of mutual confidence in the social life. This social function of norms or ideals is so important that there is always strong social pressure on people to conform.

However, one has to admit that all members of the society do not conform their behaviour and way of life to the social norms. It is also noticed that the same person changes his behaviour in different times and environments either to adjust himself with the new situation or to gain some personal benefits in the same social environment. Again it is found that all social norms are not rigid. Certain norms are changeable according to the changes in the environment. Significantly, the society itself is not static, it is dynamic. Therefore, although the members of a society conform to the norms most of the time, it is difficult to deny the possibility of violations of these norms by some members while leading a social life. In the case of certain norms, the folkways, a fair amount of non-conformity may be tolerated but in the case of certain other norms, the mores, very little scope for flexibility is noticed.

The norms of a society are ultimately an expression of its values—socially shared ideas about what is good, right, and desirable. The difference between values and norms is that values are abstract, whereas norms are behavioural rules or guidelines for people in particular kinds of situations.[11]

All cultures share a commonality of basic values that are the foundation of global ethics. Global ethics are not the imposition of "Western" values on the rest of the world. To think so would be both artificially restrictive of the scope of global ethics. The principal source of global ethics is the idea of human vulnerability and desire to alleviate the suffering of every individual to the extent possible. Another source is the belief in the basic moral equality of all human beings. The injunction to treat others as we want to be treated finds explicit mention in Buddhism, Christianity, Confucianism, Hinduism, Islam, Judaism, Taoism and Zoroastrianism, and it is implicit in other faiths.

It is on the basis of these common teachings across all cultures that states have come together to endorse the Universal Declaration of Human Rights, supported by the International Covenants on Civil and Political Rights and on Economic and Social Rights. Regional Treaties, such as the European Convention for the Protection of Human Rights, the American Convention of Human Rights and the African Charter on Human and People's Rights have taken similar initiatives. More recently, the UN's Millennium Declaration, adopted by the full membership of the General Assembly in 2000, recommended itself to human rights, fundamental freedoms and respect for equal rights to all without distinction.

There are five core elements of global ethics:

- *Equity*: Recognizing the equality of all individuals regardless of class, race, gender, community or generation is the ethos of universal values. Equity also envelops the need to preserve the environment and natural resources that can be used by future generations.
- *Human Rights and Responsibilities:* Human rights are an indispensable standard of international conduct. The basic concern is to protect the integrity of all individuals from threats to freedom and equality. The focus on individual rights acknowledges their expression on equity between individuals, which outweighs any claim made on behalf of group and collective values. But with rights come duties: bonds without options are oppressive; options without bonds are anarchy.
- *Democracy*: Democracy serves multiple ends: providing political autonomy, safeguarding individual rights and creating conditions for full participation of citizens in economic development. At the global level democratic standards are essential for ensuring participation and giving voice to poor countries, marginalized communities and discriminated against minorities.
- *Protection of Minorities*: Discrimination against minorities occurs at several levels: non-recognition, denial of political rights, socio-economic exclusion and violence. Global ethics cannot be comprehensive unless minorities receive recognition and equal rights within a larger national and global community. The promotion of tolerance is central to the process.
- *Peaceful conflict resolution and fair negotiation*: Justice and fairness cannot be achieved by imposing pre-conceived moral principles. Resolution of disagreements must be sought through negotiations. All parties deserve a say. Global ethics does not mean a single path towards peace or development or modernization. It is a framework within which societies can find peaceful solutions to problems."[12]

Shirin Ebadi, the winner of Nobel Peace Prize also said, "People are different, and so are their cultures; people live in different ways, and civilizations also differ; people speak in a variety of languages; people are guided by different religions; people are born with different colours, and many traditions influence their lives with varying colours and shades; people dress differently and adapt to their environment in different ways; people express themselves differently. Music, literature and art reflect different styles as well. But, despite these differences, all people have one single common attribute: they are all human beings—nothing more, nothing less. And, however, different they may be all cultures embrace certain common principles. No culture tolerates the exploitation of human beings. No religion allows the killing of the innocent. No civilization accepts violence or terror. Torture is abhorrent to the human conscience. Brutality and cruelty are appalling in every tradition.

In short, these common principles, which are shared by all civilizations, reflect our fundamental human rights. These rights are treasured and cherished by everyone, everywhere.

So cultural relativity should never be used as a pretext to violate human rights, since these rights embody most fundamental values of human civilizations. The Universal Declaration of Human Rights is needed universally, applicable to both East and West. It is compatible with every faith and religion. Failing to respect our human rights only undermines our humanity. Let us not destroy this fundamental truth; if we do, the weak will have nowhere to turn."[13]

Religion: Every religion consists of certain beliefs and practices. It is noticed that almost all religions focus certain similar beliefs, though in many others they differ too. Generally, in respect of the practices, the differences seem to be more glaring than similarities. The ways of prayer, the observance of various rituals and ceremonies and such other religious practices differ from one religion to another. However, there is an underlying similarity in spirit and all these practices in their own distinctive ways are directed towards God or Gods. This is the ultimate destination. It is nothing but to secure gracefulness of man's life and to be free from various kinds of suffering in the world. The influence of geographical and cultural traditions of the societies compels the members to maintain differences in the ways of religious practices.

However, there are a few striking similarities. For example, fasting is taken as a very important religious practice in most religions, such as Hinduism, Buddhism, Jainism and Islam. Similarly, the fire-worship is regarded as very sacred in both Hinduism and Zoroastrianism, pilgrimage is given a great religious value in both Hinduism and Islam. There are striking similarities between Islam and Judaism on the one hand and Judaism and Christianity on the other in respect of many other religious practices. The Christianity also insists that true religion consists in nothing but loving God as well as one's fellow beings in utmost sincerity and humility. Although a sincere moral life of love is sufficient for man's redemption, simple prayer to God without any rituals and sacrifices is also taught in Christianity. Again, reciting of religious texts is regarded as a very important religious duty in almost all the religions. Similarly, every religion gives credence to the erection of religious temples and shrines where people go either individually or in groups to pay their respect and devotion to God.

There is, however, a very clear and definite similarity in the nature of the ethical practices that the different religions prescribe. There is no such religion which teaches enmity with others, teaches excessive attachment to worldly objects as desirable. On the other hand, every religion without exception teaches the observance of such ethical virtues as liberty, humility, chastity, purity, love, kindness, truth etc. to be the sacred duty of every religious man. All religions without exception teach universal brotherhood. Similarly, all of them teach abstention from cruelty to creatures. There may be the difference of emphasis, but that does not affect the inner similarity of conviction. Sometimes, the similarity is very direct and obvious. The three religions—Hinduism, Buddhism and Jainism—assert with equal emphasis on the desirability of the observance of five ethical virtues—non-violence, truth, celibacy, non-stealing and non-attachment. An obvious similarity may be marked between the religions of Indian tradition on the one hand and Zoroastrianism on the other inasmuch as all of these equally emphasize the need for observing rightness of thought speech and action all together.[14]

The study of the religions shows that almost all the religions spell out ethical principles in very clear terms. These principles are necessary for the physical and mental health of the individuals as well as the society. These are very strong threads to tie up different communities together and to move towards the same direction with different modes of movement. These ethical principles are the devices used by different religions to assert human values in a society and these may also be considered as motivating factors to render service to humanity. Humanism is the supreme religion—religion of all the religions. It is also a significant part of Indian culture. The religions are the torch bearers to direct activities and thought of a man towards service to humanity. The welfare of mankind requires guidance or control of human power over the application of modern sophisticated technology. Survival of mankind depends only on the authority of human power over the application of technology for the progress of a society. It is a human power which can contribute to put an end to the process of dehumanization in the modern democracy.

However, the humanism may be distinguished from religion. Though man is a religious animal, both religion and humanism view man's life from different angles. Humanism is defined in the *Oxford Dictionary* as "any system of thought or action which is concerned with merely human interests or with those of the human race in general. For humanism service to man is the highest religion as man is supreme in existence in the world. It believes in the good life, in moderation, harmony, balance.

Humanism is a legitimate protest against those forms of religion which separate the secular and sacred, divide time and eternity and break up the unity of soul and flesh. Every religion should have sufficient respect for the dignity of man and the rights of human personality.

Referring to religion and social relations Radhakrishnan said religion is confused with the mechanical participation in the rites or passive acquiescence in the dogmas. Today it is found that many people visit temples, celebrate religious festivals, offer prayer to Gods and Goddesses of their faith, but their behaviour in daily life or in social relationship the spirit of religion is not reflected. The modern Indians in most cases are moving towards rituals instead of going to the depth or the core meaning of the religion they profess. This is very common among the youth.

In a new society we need a new universal reliance of religion. By it we mean not a uniform religion but a religion of awareness and love, of wisdom and compassion, of truth and love.

Tolerance is also very important factor in religion for establishing peace and harmony in the society. Tolerance implies an elementary right belonging to the dignity of every man. The right to believe like the right to live a free, unfettered life is fundamental to the concept of brotherly love. We have had in our country peaceful co-existence of different religions. It is not mere passive co-existence but an active fellowship, a close inter-relation of the best of different religions. We have not adhered steadfastly to these ideals and have suffered often. Yet the ideal has been kept in view and supported by great leaders like Ram Mohun Roy, Rama Krishna, Tagore and Gandhiji.

Each religion is unique so far as its form is concerned. We can hold that our particular formulation is valid formulation of truth without denying the validity of other forms. We must develop those loyalties to the free mind and spirit which transcend the narrower loyalties to the caste or class, race or nation. Whatever progress we make at the cost of these values is morally wrong.

True religion is not the religion of routine which we adopt as a matter of habit. It is the aspiration of every human soul, that which unfolds within oneself, that which is built by one's life blood. It is the fulfilment of our nature in which overflows into the world's service.[15]

Folkways and Norms: Norms ensure that social life proceeds smoothly, for they give guidelines for our own behaviour and reliable expectations for behaviour of others.

The codes are nothing but norms to ensure that social life is peaceful and secured. For they give us guidelines within the frame work of which individuals have to behave and these codes help establishment and promotion of mutual confidence in the society. This social function of norms is so important that there is always strong social pressure on people to conform. However, one has to admit that all members of the society do not conform their behaviour and way of life to the social norms. It is also noticed that the same person changes his behaviour in different times and environments either to adjust himself with new situation or to gain some personal benefits in the same social environment. Again, it is found that all social norms are not rigid. Certain norms are changeable according to the changes in the environment. Society itself is not static, it is dynamic. Therefore, although the members of a society conform to the norms most of the time it is difficult to deny the possibility of violations of these norms by some members while leading a social life. In the case of certain norms, the folkways, a fair amount of non-conformity may be tolerated but in the case of others, the mores, very little scope for flexibility is noticed.

Human Rights and Human Dignity: The concept of human rights is a great contribution of human thought to the culture and civilization of every nation. It is flourishing at every stage of the progress of human civilization embracing new areas of man's interest. Gradually, human rights are developing in different dimensions.[16]

The dynamic nature of the concept of human rights is reflected in the definition offered by Harold J. Laski in his book, *Grammar of Politics*, when he said, "rights are those conditions of social life without which no man can seek to be himself." It indicates wide meaning and evolutionary character of the concept. Similar is the case when Professor Hobhouse put it as, "rights are what we expect from others and others from us and all genuine rights are conditions of social welfare." Here addition has been made of the relationship between the rights and duties. Gandhi also asserted that the true source of right is duty. The rights are required not only for development of personality of an individual but also to fulfil the social responsibilities of an individual.[17]

Any discussion on human rights cannot be divorced from its normative aspect of connotation. Social Sciences are normative sciences and as a part of social sciences human rights set certain norms or ideals for establishing a peaceful society. At the same time these rights are supported by the norms of the society. These are nothing but moral principles that set out certain standards of human behaviour and regularly protected as legal rights in national and international laws. They are commonly understood as inalienable Fundamental Rights to which a person is inherently entitled simply because she or he is human being.[18]

From the above it is found that human rights are inherent to all human beings whatever their nationality, place of residence, sex, national or ethnic origin, colour, religion, language, or any other status. All are equally entitled to their human rights without discrimination. These rights are all interrelated, interdependent and indivisible.[19]

Human rights are the claims of an individual for the realization of human qualities, which the nature has bestowed on him or her as human being.

The concept of human rights is closely connected to human dignity. The principles of human rights constitute a strong device to ensure protection of dignity of each and every individual in the society. This also invites equal respect and development of human qualities, such as, intelligence, talent and conscience and satisfaction of spiritual needs.[20]

Aung San Suu Kyi, winner of Nobel Peace Prize in 1991, said, "respect for human dignity implies commitment to creating conditions under which individual can develop a sense of self-worth and security. True dignity comes with an assurance of one's ability to rise to the challenges of the human situation. Such assurance is unlikely to be fostered in people who have to live with the threat of violence and injustice, with bad governance and instability or with poverty and disease. Eradicating of these threats must be the aim of those who recognize the sanctity of human dignity and of those who strive to promote human development. Development as growth, advancement and the realization of potential depends on available resources – and no resource is more potential than people empowered by confidence in their value as human beings."[21]

Dignity provides a sense of value. The human rights and their observance may be considered as an indicator of awareness of an individual of the dignity of others and thus adherence of human values. Self-realization is not possible in isolation of social life because it is a part of common humanity.[22]

Human rights entail both rights and obligations. In modern democracy States assume obligations and duties under international law to respect, to protect and to fulfill human rights. The obligation to respect means that states must refrain from interfering with or curtailing the enjoyment of human rights. The obligation to protect requires states to protect individuals and groups against human rights abuses. The obligation to fulfil means that states must take positive action to facilitate the enjoyment of basic human rights. At the individual level, when we are entitled to our human rights, we should respect the human rights of others.[23]

The above discussion reflects the universal character of the doctrine of human rights. However, the universal character of human rights cannot do away with the diversity that exists in the global human society. Canely and Jones stated clearly that the universality of these rights has to be safeguarded in a world characterized by diversity—a world in which people live in different circumstances, bear different cultures, profess different religions, and pursue different ways of life. Further, human individuals exhibit different physical and personal characteristics. They also exhibit differences as members of different societies and professions. These differences do not stand as a hindrance to accept the universal character of human rights. Simple reason for it is that in spite of these differences the truth is that all are human beings. The social values, customs and traditions differ from country to country and in the same country amongst different communities. India has the experience of the diversity in beliefs and values adhered by different ethnic groups which have affected the human rights of individuals. For a long time the doctrine of human rights was not asserted by certain sections of the Indians, especially in the rural and hill areas who gave priority to the social customs and traditions to human rights.[24]

Without respect for human rights social life is not possible because it requires mutual respect for each other, fellow-feeling, co-existence of differences of opinion etc. United Nations has made efforts for spreading the human rights education by creating a separate establishment.

Human Rights education and teaching aim at:

(i) Fostering the attitudes of tolerance, respect and solidarity inherent in human rights;
(ii) Providing knowledge about human rights, in both their national and international dimensions, and the institutions established for their implementation; and
(iii) Developing the individual's awareness of the ways and means by which human rights can be translated into social and political reality at both the national and international levels.

Further it was also suggested that human rights must be seen as an aspect of professional, ethical and social responsibility in all fields of research, study, teaching and work.[25]

Relationship between Ethics and Human Rights: The interdependence of human rights and ethical principles is an undeniable fact. The ethical principles constitute a strong device to safeguard human rights while laws of a country can create an environment for generating inner power to realize the strength and significance of these principles in the global human family. The tragic events, worst and violent situations faced by different nations in the path of progress of human civilization create confusion in the minds of the people making them frustrated and indecisive to confirm their faith on the human power and to adopt ethical or moral principles in his way of life. The progress of science and technology helps the indecisive man to move from the stage of indecisiveness towards acquiring decision making power to stabilize his shaky mind and he tries to confirm his belief on the irrelevance of moral or ethical principles in the modern civilization or his modern way of life. But, we must remember that unless the use of scientific products is directed by human power for the service to humanity the safeguard of human rights will remain as a slogan only causing severe damage to humanity itself. Human rights may also be considered as a very strong thread to unite different nations in the world, different communities in a nation, different families in a community and different members within the same family passing through different multicolour social cultures.

Kofi Anan said, "In the 21st century I believe that the mission of the United Nations will be defined by a new, more profound awareness of the sanctity and dignity of every human life, regardless of race or religion. This will require us to look beyond the framework of states and beneath the surface of nations and communities. We must focus, as never before, on improving the conditions of the individual men and women who give the state or nation its richness and character."[26]

While talking about the space of ethics and human values in the socio-political life of a nation one has to admit that modern India occupies a unique position in the contemporary world due to contributions made by Mahatma Gandhi to this concept. Gandhiji bridged the gap between individual and social ethics and regarded social reality as a counterpart of man's inner reality. To him individual freedom had a value but one must not, he said, "forget that man is essentially a social being. He has risen to present status by learning to adjust his individualism to the requirements of social progress."[27]

Gandhi was successful to make heartfelt appeal not only to the enlightened people of the country but also illiterate and innocent people of all parts of the country to observe the principle of non-violence and to be *Styagrahi* during freedom movement. To Gandhi there must be non-violence in the private life itself. He learnt it from the Jainist traditions of non-violence, his saintly mother, disciplined father and tolerant wife. Non-violence helps one to develop the inner strength, the soul force necessary for the *Satyagrahi*. A *Satyagrahi* is a man of peace. Positively, a *Satyagrahi* will always try to overcome evil by good, anger by love, untruth by truth, *himsa* by *ahimsa*.

It is also a way of group life. *Satyagraha* fights violence among groups. Gandhi points out that anything that millions can do together becomes charged with a unique power of *Satyagraha*. A *Satyagraha* needs a leader, who is the very soul of mass *Satyagraha*. The leader should have sterling qualities. The most important of these are:

(a) Sincerity and all-embracing love;
(b) Culture and dignified bearing;
(c) Self-control;
(d) Selflessness;
(e) Pursuit of non-possession;
(f) Rooted in the soil of and having the spirit of *Swdeshi;* and
(g) Faith in God which is synonymous with truth should be unshakable.[28]

To be a true servant of the people he must be the possessor of above qualities. Because these qualities make a man human. Human society can be served effectively only by a human being not by a half-human being or by an animal, just as only the democrats can make democratic way of life successful.[29]

The aim of Gandhi was to seek truth. In seeking truth he wanted to see how he could be of the greatest use to humanity. He pointed out several times that the "greatest good of all" and not the "good of the majority" is to be sought. To Gandhi means and ends must be pure. The reason is that end grows out means. That which is achieved by chicanery, bribery, deceit is transitory. Good means, alone, it was believed by Gandhi, can achieve lasting peace and progress. But a question that arises is how this can be achieved. Gandhi said:

1. Self-realization in which the individual examines himself;
2. Self-purification; and
3. Ethical discipline in which the individual follows certain laid out principles.

He points out, "he who is not prepared to order his life in unquestionable obedience to the laws of morality cannot be said to be a man in the full sense of the word." Therefore he advocated certain moral vows."[30]

The essence of entire concept of Gandhian philosophy may be conveyed in a single word: *Satyagraha*. It is also the word that has the entire Gandhian technique of action as its core. *Satyagraha* is essentially the art of confronting the opponent with a moral challenge and socio-psychological situation. It is logically impossible to deny Gandhi's contention that *Satyagraha* is the only means which can preserve and promote the values of liberty, equality and fraternity. A *Satyagrahi* is constantly training himself for assuming profound moral responsibility of changing social relationship and institutions; and in doing so he is not only refusing to violate the liberty of his adversary, but subjecting himself alone to all the suffering involved in the act of *Satyagraha*. He is thus acting as a free agent with individual moral responsibility as well as allowing his adversary to act in a similar manner. Secondly, since the whole basis of *Satyagraha* is the recognition of the relativity of values and the essential equality of all human beings, it preserves and promotes equality in a very real sense. The *Satyagrahi* confronts his adversary fearlessly, to the extent of sacrificing his life in the confrontation, and looks him in the eye as equal, not as inferior or superior. Finally, fraternity and wider love is the very essence of *Satyagraha*. *Satyagrahi* covers neither power nor dominance either for himself or for his party or class, but is interested solely in securing justice, and is constantly training himself not to bear ill will for the adversary, he is an embodiment of fraternity although he is determined to extinguish the system for which his opponent is responsible. Indeed fraternity is the first principle of *Satyagraha* and all other considerations are secondary.[31]

An individual is an agent of social transformation. For this, according to Gandhi, control of the self-interest of the individual is an essential prerequisite to transform the social relationships in terms of ultimate values. The values inculcated in the individual before they can find true social expression. He emphasized the need of a private moral effort on the part of the individual before he can qualify for social action.[32]

Man has the duty to care for others. This is possible only through the development of moral qualities of an individual. A moral man always attempts to accommodate the interest of the society. While recognizing mutual interdependence between individual and society Gandhi did not talk merely of functional-interdependence, he embraced within it the value of harmony, integration of self with humanity also. The harmony between individual and society is a dynamic process. It evolves through clash of personality, interchange of opinion and exchange of ideas. Thus the society is based on extended self of individuals, harmony, non-exploitation, equality and participation.

According to Gandhi 'inner Voice' is the conscience of an individual. He also said the 'inner voice' of self-disciplined individual is not contrary to basic moral principles. Morality includes, as Gandhi said, nobleness of character, purity of soul and motive, the notions of truth, selfless service and goodness of means. A moral man always adopt moral principles for the solution of the problems—personal or social. We can have a dream of new human world when mutual relationship of the individuals depends on understanding of moral values of humanity. Full development of moral character can make a man perfect to the maximum level.

A peaceful disposition of the whole personality is indispensable for moral life. Because tranquility, calmness and mild temperament help development of morality. Gandhi said, "freedom from bad habits forms another element of morality." Habit is nothing but capacity or tendency of an individual resulting from repetition of the same act. A man is considered as good or bad on the basis of his or her habits.

Every man has reasoning capacity. With this power an individual can decide what is right and what is wrong. An individual with good habit or moral habit will be guided in a positive and constructive way. This will help development of the concept of 'inner voice' within him. When individual becomes matured in thought and action based on moral values, then he or she will be empowered by 'soul force'.[33]

The freedom movement in India under the leadership of Gandhiji may be called as a process of democratization of the society because he tried to humanize the whole concept of democracy through the movement. He realized that every human institution is prone to danger. Therefore, the people must be alert and sensitive to humanize it by putting it in the right direction. To quote Gandhi:

> "There is no human institution that has not its dangers. The greater the institution, the greater chances of abuse. Democracy is an institution and therefore, it is liable to be greatly abused. The remedy, therefore, is not avoidance of Democracy but reduction of possibility of abuse to a minimum."[34]

Gandhi accepted democracy as a way of life. He was anxious to establish democratic values. Preservation of such values can only bring about a new social order where "all for one and one for all" can truly function. It is a vast programme of mass education. But the democratic educators must also display the democratic values in their way of life. The people are not attracted through simple prophecy only. According to Gandhiji, the essence of democratic way of life is that individuals must have mutual respect and sympathy for each other. Each individual shall keep his fellow man ahead of him in respect of enjoying social responsibilities. This retrospective desire to stand for each other's cause will create an atmosphere of social responsibilities. To Gandhi social justice and individual freedom do not stand in contrary to each other. Their aims and objectives are same. Discipline and restraint in the life of individual will only help him to achieve the social well being. In the words of Gandhiji:

> "A born democrat is a born disciplinarian. Democracy comes naturally to him who is habituated normally to yield willing obedience to all laws, human or divine...let those

> who are ambitious to serve democracy qualify themselves first the acid test of democracy. Moreover a democrat must be utterly selfless. He must think or dream not in terms of self or party but only of democracy..."[35].

Gandhi talked of several kinds of freedom. The significant of those are as below:

Personal Freedom: When a man voluntarily takes decisions, expresses his nature spontaneously through his own thought, word and deed, he is said to possess personal freedom.

Moral Freedom: When a man, obeying the dictates of the inner voice, acts voluntarily by sticking to truth and non-violence and feels responsibility for his chosen actions, he is said to enjoy moral freedom.

Social Freedom: When a man voluntarily takes decisions, adjusts himself with all environments and sets himself free from all social restraints for the good of all, he is said to enjoy social freedom.

A man who enjoys social freedom will always be free from restraints like narrow casteism, nepotism, regionalism, traditions like untouchability, child marriages etc.

Economic Freedom: When a man voluntarily takes decisions, adjusts himself with all economic environments and sets himself free from all economic constraints for the good of all, he is said to be enjoying economic freedom.

A man who enjoys economic freedom will always live with minimum material wants. His life will be guided by need but not by greed. His economic life will be free from inside or outside competition and exploitation which come due to the unnecessary production, consumption, exchange and distribution.

Political Freedom: When a man voluntarily takes decisions, adjusts with all political environments and sets himself free from all political restraints for the good of all, he is said to be enjoying political freedom.

A man who enjoys political freedom will always live a life of self-rule. He admits the rule of the state which has least rules. His political life will be free from the cheap mentalities, giving authority to a few, ruling of the brute majority and copying the rule of foreign countries.

Lovers of Freedom always take the responsibility for the proper functioning of the government. When each member of the community discharges his duties, he contributes something to the welfare of all. The shirking of duties by individuals definitely leads to the imbalanced growth of the society. The strength of each member is the strength of a nation. This strength lies in his duties but not in mere rights. Thus, the freedom aims at establishing good governance by training each individual as a responsible citizen.[36]

The law of truth, according to Gandhi does not merely refer to truth in speech, it also refers to truth in action and truth in thought. Truth has reference to all spheres of life of a man. If he fails to practice this principle, he departs from the path of truth, denies the soul in himself. Truth rules out prejudices, evasion, secrecy and deception as well as exaggeration, suppression or modification of reality. Truth helps mutual toleration and avoidance of dogmatism and bitterness. Gandhi also advocated that while speaking the truth one should take care that it is not bitter. Truth must be accompanied by non-violence. However, non-violent truth does not mean hypocrisy, even every harsh truth can be communicated courteously and gently.

India gained Independence on 15th August, 1947 from colonial rule after a long struggle under the leadership of Mahatma Gandhi, whose ideals of non-violence is well respected throughout the world even now. The process of the struggle for independence of India may be traced with the efforts of Mahatma Gandhi to fight for human rights in South Africa. Throughout the long struggle he devoted to the cause of human rights of the Indians through *Satyagraha* and Non-violence. He could mobilize even the Indian women to come out of the four walls of their habitation to participate in the movement. The non-cooperation movement which was a major component of the freedom struggle could embrace even the young students of the country.

The old values which were adhered by the Indians during ancient, medieval and initial stage of independent India continued to play a significant role in the socio-political life of the country. However, with the spread of education, development of communication facilities, recently with the development of information technology, emergence of globalization cause change of values in our society. More weight age is attached on enhancement of material possession and money power. While enriching money power man does not care to set aside the standing values like doing no harm to others, showing due respect to human dignity, to avoid unethical activities etc. The main reasons for this state of affair in the country may be power of money in occupying respectable position in the society, to secure employment, to get admission in the professional institutions for study etc. People today, do not hesitate to adopt all kinds of unethical devices and to distort old Indian values required for the establishment of peace and harmony in the society and to make progress of the nation. The concept of *Dharma* as enshrined in the *Manusmriti* and other ethical values constituting the core area of each religion of the world has been dethroned from the world of religion. The superfluous rituals in the religious occasions have become very strong commanding force to attract the people of all ages in the country.

In the language of Radhakrishnan "gaining independence has been a simpler task compared with the one of administering the country in a clean, decent way." This seems to be more formidable task. For it we require selfless leadership, an honest and competent civil service. We require a disciplined military and police force. We require expert industrial managers and skilled workers and good agricultural peasants. Our ordinary citizens should have civic sense and national feeling.

All these things cannot be achieved in a day. What we are attempting to do to our best of our power is to take some steps towards developing a sound administration, a stable government and a healthy nation. We cannot say that we are satisfied with what we have done. There are things happening in different parts of the country which make us feel sad, depressed and ashamed of ourselves. What is necessary is the strong sense of patriotism. It is true that we developed a negative kind of patriotism when we struggled to rid of the country of foreign rule (What we do not want: Foreign rule). But a positive patriotism, a dynamic fellow-feeling, a sense of belonging to this country, of being proud to belong to it, these things yet to come. We have to build these in the minds and hearts of men.[37]

We fought for Independence with a desire to develop a democratic set-up in the society. Democracy has three basic dimensions—political, economic and social. Political and economic democracy are rooted in social democracy. Social democracy has been said by Mahatma Gandhi as a way of life. It is not merely a way of life but an ethical way of life. Nobody could deny it and recently the Indian scholars have started discussing about good governance in the country. The government did not make any explicit pronouncement of it nor the course of actions of the government reflects it till recently. Only the government led by Narenda Modi as Prime Minister made explicit pronouncement of it when it said, "Minimum government and maximum governance". Here lies the need of ethical way of life. As Radhakrishnan said, "Democracy is a faith." It is a faith on human power as well as intellectual power. The concept of maximum governance also demands freedom which means restraints. Once a man restraints himself from encroaching upon other's freedom there emerges humility of man which is the core element of good governance. Good governance is nothing but democratic or self- governance.

Those who won freedom for India and created its constitutional systems were, like the founding fathers of the United States' Constitution, men of rare talent and dedication. One point of similarity, and perhaps the greatest, between the constitutions of the world's two largest democracies is their high moral tone.

Acharya J.B. Kripalani spoke eloquently in the Constituent Assembly on17th October, 1949, "I want this House to remember that what we have enunciated are not merely legal, constitutional and formal principles, but moral principles; and moral principles have to be lived, whether it is in private life, or it is public life, whether it is in commercial life, political life or the life of an administrator. They have to be lived throughout."[38]

The Constitution of India reflects the Indian culture very well. It was formulated at the instance of galaxy of eminent Indians under the chairmanship of Dr. Rajendra Prasad. Dr. B.R. Ambedkar was the Chairman of the Drafting Committee. Under their leadership other eminent Indians participated in the task of preparation of the Constitution. The Preamble to the Constitution focuses on moral and human values and inclusiveness of all in governance of the country through the phrase, "We, the People of India."[39]

The Preamble to the Constitution of India lays emphasis upon the maintenance of the dignity of the individual for establishment of fraternity or brotherhood. Towards this end fundamental rights of the citizens have been provided so that each individual can get an opportunity to be developed as human person. The violation of fundamental rights invites a serious threat to human dignity. It is also noticed that the framers of the Constitution realized that it is not enough to make the fundamental rights justiciable unless he is free from economic wants and misery. Dr. Radhakrishnan in his speech at a seminar on Parliamentary Democracy on 25th February, 1956 said, "Poor people who wander about, find no work, no wages and starve, whose lives are continual round of sore affliction and pinching poverty, cannot be proud of the constitution and its law." As a result of it the Directive Principles of State Policy have been incorporated in the Part IV of the Constitution of India, exhorting the State to shape its social and economic policies in such a manner that "all citizens, men and women equally, have the right to an adequate means of livelihood," "just and humane conditions of work"(Article 42) and "a decent standard of life and full enjoyment of leisure and social and cultural opportunities."[40]

Unfortunately, in India the divisive forces on the basis of caste, community is assuming alarming nature. The social, political, administrative institutions which have to take the leading role in establishing mutual faith in establishing harmony amongst social groups professing different religious faiths, practicing different social cultures, speaking different languages, are almost collapsing and not in a position to command the confidence of the citizens of independent India and the question of taking the leading role in establishing peace, harmony, mutual faith in the society does not arise. In other words, India's glorious past with rich culture and civilization is in threat of disappearing.

Here mention may also be made of what Guy B. Adams and Danny L. Balfour talked about ethical failure in their article, titled, "Ethical Failings, Incompetence, and Administrative Evil". Incompetence and greed are the two major sources of ethical failure in public administration. Both of them made an attempt to bring out a relationship between incompetence and ethical failure by saying that both combining together may lead to serious wrong things.[41]

Gandhi's principles provided the scope for acquiring moral strength of the people during struggle for freedom of the country.

His style of living and social relationship and committed service to the freedom of the individuals as well as the nation remind us every moment that mere material progress cannot bring human progress. Human progress must be grounded on human values. Gandhi realized it and accordingly, he made human approach for bringing social change.

Here mention may be made of what Herbert Spencer thought of social change. To him social progress is divergent, moving in different directions touching different areas of man's life. In this process each element of change gives birth to new elements inviting new approach or modification of existing approach. Naturally, there arises multiplicity of changing elements making social life complex day by day. The process of social reform must address all the elements. Because each element is active in its own way in the society and different persons may give different weight age to these elements according to their personal or individual interest overlooking the social interest. To Professor Ellwood the material as well as moral development emerges only from this process. But, the problem of modifying the social life is essentially a problem of modifying habits in the masses of individuals and therefore our efforts have to be made in the direction of combined growth of individuals as well as the masses. Gandhi also realized that to uproot exploitation from the society the exploiter must change his heart. He preferred social service as an instrument for establishment of an exploitation free society and if it fails then one should take the help of Satyagraha.[42]

To reduce all pervasive criminalization in all forms of ethical aspect of all religions must be brought to light and the children must be made aware of it through theory and practice of education process of the country. The moral code should be emphasized in all institutions to make them effective in rendering service to humanity. Since in the ultimate analysis of institutions there remains the human beings and morality is the human related problem. The ethical principles and human values contribute significantly to make a nation strong.[43] We have to keep up our struggle against the inertia and evil in us. All our enemies are within us. The impulses which seduce, the flames which burn, spring from the inner region of ignorance and error in which we live. Man's glory is not in never falling but in rising every time he falls. Professor A.N. Whitehead says, "religion is a force of belief cleansing the inward parts. For this reason the primary religious virtue is sincerity, a penetrating sincerity. Religion is art and theory of the internal life of man. The way from passion to peace is by self-conquest. The measure of a man's saintliness is judged by the degree to which he has been able to overcome the frailties of his nature. Religion is not a way out of life but a way unto life. The general assumption that Hinduism negates social values and sacrifices material and cultural needs to a world—negating spiritual quest is not correct. It is true that when we have the vision of reality, we feel that we are strangers in the outer, visible, alien world of appearance. We do not feel at home.[44] Referring to modern technological civilization Radhakrishnan in his writings very clearly stated that in a technological civilization the individuals become depersonalized social units. Things control life, statistical averages replace qualitative human beings. To be human is to be trusting, to be kind, to be cooperative, to be sympathetic and responsive. We must recover our humanity from the scourge depersonalization or dehumanization of individuals in the modern technological civilization to establish good governance and then only corruption may be reduced.

From the above discussion it may be said that social, administrative and political ailments require moral or ethical therapy along with rules and regulations, punishment and structural and functional reforms of administration. Corruption is appearing in the contemporary as serious ailments in the fields of politics, administration and society as a whole to achieve good governance in the modern democracy. Corruption is a very strong and destructive force to the society. It is an indicator of ethical vacuity in a man. Good governance is a right answer to corruption which is appearing as a challenge to the modern world. Good governance is a moral concept and therefore, every actor, i.e. individual must be equipped with moral power. Here notable point is that this power cannot be imposed from outside nor it can be acquired through imitation from others. To be morally strong an individual must have the opportunity to develop his personality. Personality of an individual refers to the ways of thought, feeling, social adjustment and behaviour consistently exhibited over time that strongly influences one's expectations, self-perceptions, values and attitudes.

Contemporary India is experiencing conflicting ideas and

ideals in the process of transformation of the society. Today the problems of our country range from the urgent necessity to the eternal questions of history. Further, corruption and crimes have become omnipresent. Mutual distrust, hatred towards each other, violation of human rights, exploitation through fake financial and educational institutions, hypocrisy etc. have become common problems in modern India. The cities or urban areas are full of exploiters, violators of laws in the country causing deterioration of the law and order situation to a large extent. Threat is occurring to the survival of human society as well as the animal world. This situation reminds us what the Haldane Committee of Britain observed in 1918 that Britain had no arrangement or provision for systematic application of thought as to the policy formulation and implementation. Very often doubt arises whether we are also facing the same situation in India today. It is difficult to deny that the flaws in the government policy-making process may cause serious damage to a democratic country. However, the political leadership in India is itself aware of the problems in administration caused by rampant corruption in the country and this awareness is evident in its efforts to bring to light the various forms of corruption in the country and the steps to take action against the persons involved in it. The Government, while trying to utilize the modern skill and knowledge of the scientists, technologists and planners, must make every effort to see that they work within the ethical framework. It must also try to create an environment for revival of ancient traditional wisdom for the solution of certain problems. We cannot afford to deviate from the human culture of traditional India while taking measures for development and modernization of the society. In this situation we have to realize that a democratic society is not one that ignores individual differences but one that deals with them wisely and humanely through public policy.

Education is a right answer to any human malady. Corruption is a very serious human malady. It can be cured by human medicine. Notably, its impact is deep rooted in the mind of an individual. Lord Macaulay, the British reformer of civil service and who was in India as Governor General said that an educated man is also a moral man. Therefore, there is no need to have a moral test of any educated man. But, experience in India is other way round. In India, especially in states like Assam highly educated persons belonging to administration and educational institutions are alleged to be corrupted in various ways. These are communicated almost every day by both print media as well as e-media. It indicates the failure of education to achieve its ultimate goal. Its journey is up to award of marks to be competent enough to stand in the que for a job. In short educational institutions have failed to provide right kind of education. V.R. Krishna Iyer, in his book, "*Justice and Beyond*" stated, "Right type of education is creative, not destructive, soulful not soulless." Corrupt generation reflects the character of education divorced from its basic value-man making. Until man becomes human through education the human society is in peril. Education, to justify itself, should enable a man to use the full potential of his body, mind and spirit. Those who are in the process of education must see that the spirit of enquiry, the joy of discovery, the urge for expression, the objectivity of experiment and the pursuit of investigative truth are inculcated in the mind of students through the process of education. Creativity and originality justify the supreme worth of the human person and this is how attempt may be made to make a man moral. Through this type of education one can get out of dark rust of mental inactivity and idleness caused by modern technological civilization.[45]

What was the apprehension of Dr. Ambedkar has become true. Today India is facing acute dearth of honest and dedicated manpower. Almost every service is crying for moral leadership. Ethical principles have been thrown out, well established Indian tradition has been distorted in the name of modernization. Bribery which is the common form of corruption is appearing as a deadly weapon to destroy India's age old human tradition. Gaps and flows of the Constitution have become convenient devices to satisfy the selfish interests of the service providers. Commitment to the cause of the nation and the goals of the Constitution of India is neither honoured nor adhered by the people. Under this situation human rights of the people are not safe. Best way to cultivate human culture in the existing situation is to sensitize the significance of human rights education through both formal and informal ways of group life so that effective approach may be made to eradicate deadly diseases like corruption.

The aims of human rights education are:

(a) To strengthen respect for human rights and fundamental freedoms;
(b) To develop fully the human personality and the sense of human dignity;
(c) To promote understanding and tolerance among diverse national, ethnic, religious and linguistic groups; and
(d) To empower people to participate actively in social activities.

The aims of human rights education are reflected in a definition adopted by UNESCO's International Congress on Education of Human Rights and Democracy in 1993 as "Human rights education is a human right, a precondition for sustainable development, the civil, social and democracy." It was also accepted that "human rights education provide protection from discrimination, unfair treatment, undemocratic attitude, deterioration of cultural values, exploitation, bondage, human rights illiteracy, abuses of human rights at any level."[46]

Any strategy to curb unethical behaviour and corruption must address, mainly three issues—Good Governance; Education and Human Culture in Social Relationship.

Good governance has moral dimension with democratic values. The present world is striving to re-humanize the global society. One cannot deny that good governance is the ultimate weapon to prevent corruption and other social ailments causing hindrance to the path of human progress. Society and the Any strategy designed to combat unethical behaviour and corruption must be a deep strategy focusing on economic and institutional reforms within the ethical framework.

The concept of good governance involves all the stakeholders to fight well against unethical behaviour and corruption. The role of the civil society must be clearly defined in the strategy document. One sector is not enough to curb corruption. The strategy document should clearly allocate responsibilities for each actor in the strategy. The actors are—civil servants, politicians, private sector, local bodies, families etc. A range of tools, systems and conditions militate against undesirable conduct in public life, providing incentives that foster professionalism and higher standards of conduct in public service. The ethical infrastructure provides control, guidance, and management of ethical conduct.

Ethical infrastructure is the fundamental requirement in public life and public service.

As regards human culture I have already mention that India is well known for humaneness and calm nature of people without any harshness in their principles and ideals. Humanism may be defined as 'any system of thought or action which is concerned with merely human interests'. For humanism man is the highest type of individual in existence and the service of man is the highest religion. It believes that man is by nature good and evil rests in society, in the conditions which surround man, and if these are removed, man's goodness will emerge.[47]

Unfortunately, the erosion of the human aspect of modern democracy is mirrored very prominently since the middle of Twentieth century. On the eve of 65th Independence Day of India Pratibha Devi Singh Patil, first lady President of the country has reminded the nation that the real strength of a country is judged not by the challenges faced by it but by its responses to them. While analyzing the laws and regulations of the country one must keep in mind that the moral ideals of our society are not annihilated and one should not forget the goals of the nation. Similarly, Janaki Ballav Patnaik, Head of the state of Assam also reminded us that our new steps in the changes of the society must be in the process of humanization only. Now time has come to make an audit of human aspect of our social life, welfare efforts of the state and the responses of the state to the challenges faced by it and the responses of the people to the challenges faced by them.[48]

Who should initiate the task? The answer is family and educational institution must be initiators of the process of humanization of the society. In the family it is the mother who is the right person to initiate the process of re-humanization of our society. The task of re-inventing world democracy must begin at home at the initiative of the mother. It is the family where the mother of a child provides fundamental infrastructure for development of personality of her child as human being. A child is born with love, affection, care and attention of the mother. The mother is the protector and giver of all these to her baby with the assistance and guidance of the father and other members of the family. I have a strong belief that any person who is committed to offer motherly treatment to the children deserves the status of a mother in the democratic world of today. Because love, affection, care, and attention constitute the ethical or moral infrastructure required for democratic way of life, which are provided to them in the family itself at the early stage. In this regard it occupies a unique position in a society. A woman has to be honoured not merely as house-maker but also as builder of a democratic society. Human culture or human relationship begins at home with the warmth primarily of the mother followed by other members of the family in which a baby is born.

Family is the primary socializing institution. This institution is based on the natural love and the members are emotionally united. The children are protected and taken care of by the parents and other members by providing food, cloth, shelter and satisfying other emotional needs of the children. The most notable aspect of the child's life is the process of socialization which begins at home. The seeds of social virtues like sympathy, fellow-feeling, love and cooperation are sown in their minds by the members of the family. Family is like a cultivating field of personal and social virtues of a man. This field must be fertile for the healthy growth of the personality of a child. The children develop love and reverence for their parents, learn obeying the instructions of their parents and pick up the nature of the ways of living from the parents. The spirit of self-sacrifice and community life or mutual sharing and adjustment with brothers and sisters begins at home itself. Therefore, utmost care has to be taken by the parents not to influence their minds by narrow mental outlook or other elements like hatred to others, selfishness, ego and other cruel behaviour to others in the midst of whom the children spend most of their time.

A baby is not born with the sense of morality. It is inculcated in him through the process of socialization which begins at home. Lipi Mukhopadhyay, in her article, '*Social Conditioning and Deviant Behaviour*' rightly pointed out that a baby has no conscience and is ignorant of values. He is neither moral nor immoral. He starts learning moral codes at home from the parents followed by teachers and peer groups. Though it is a lifelong process to learn, to confirm and reconfirm the faith on these moral codes, the foundation for it is laid down in the mind of a child very well at home itself.

The baby judges what is good or bad in the context of pleasure and pain, attitude and behaviour of others towards him rather than what is right and what is wrong. Gradually, his moral codes develop in the environment of the family to which he belongs, where he spends more time and with whom he is more attached.

Family relationships play a very important role in developing the personality of the children. The emotional attachment is reflected in their behaviour to each other. The children learn things through imitation. They do not have the capacity at the early age to judge what is good or what is bad. Therefore, the elderly members of the family have to take utmost care to create healthy environment for development of personality of a child.[49]

The next is the educational institution which is deeply and directly associated with the process of socialization of the children. The teachers play a significant role in initiating the process of development of human traits in a child. They occupy a position next to the parents of the children. Thus, the responsibility of socialization of a child which begins at home is handed over to the teachers in the educational institutions. Unlike home, school is a formal institution to impart education to the children. It is to be noted that the human traits to be sustained must be rooted in the habit of the children. Therefore, both the institutions have to be associated very closely with the process of habitualization also. Thus, both parents and the teachers are inalienable parts of the processes of socialization and habitualisation of the children. It is not an easy task as the society changes and with it values also change. The traditional society is moving towards modernization or industrialization. They must see that the children carry with them at every step of their progress the human qualities. Because the movement of the traditional society towards modernization not only affects the process of socialization but also social values inviting contradictions and confusions in the minds of the youth. They also adopt certain habits through imitation without realizing the consequence of those habits. Here is the need of social awareness to build up healthy social relationship so that a concerted effort can be made to put the youth force in the right direction.

The institutions of family and school undertake heavy responsibility of making a child from being to becoming. While making them proficient in the field of their studies the educational institutions must also take care to see that they become good citizens of the country and good individuals of the society in the face of the changing world. Their thought process, behaviour, living style etc., which are shaped by the socializing agencies are reflected in their service lives.

Dr. Bhim Rao Ambedkar's concept of democracy provides first priority to social democracy to political democracy or self-rule. He did not contribute to the view that to reform the society one requires political power. Ambedkar, in his book titled, '*Ranade, Gandhi and Jinnah*' stated that it would be a serious mistake to believe that social democracy would follow political democracy and asserted that rights must exist first before power is set-up. What Ambedkar believed cannot be rejected when one looks into the existing state of politico-administrative world of India. The contemporary trend of social changes and the values asserted by the individuals as members of the society have contributed to a great extent the existing deteriorating political and administrative situation in the country. Effective and healthy political democracy can flourish only in a society which is governed by democratic and ethical principles.[50]

What is lacking today is the obedience to human values and human dignity. A new form of slavery has emerged in India caused by money and muscle power. Now the question is how to save India from this slavery and redirect the society towards humanity so that each individual can be released from the uncomfortable stay in the domain of monetary slavery. Today ethical vacuum in every walk of life is causing deviation from the real path of human progress.

Today's socio-political situation in India induces a researcher or a social scientist to think that the way of life of an Indian has to be grounded in the Indian tradition and philosophy to make the country strong and suitable for living with human dignity. While adjusting with the changes in the modern world one must be well acquainted with the Indian tradition and philosophy to serve the country successfully. Mere expertness or knowledge on a particular issue or modern technology is not enough, unless the user of modern technology is selfless, moral and sympathetic to the people.

Now, India is facing dearth of honest and dedicated manpower. What is needed, most urgently is the moral leadership at every walk of life. While modernizing the way of life we cannot afford to throw out the ethical principles nor the well established Indian Culture and tradition can be distorted by us.

REFERENCES

1. Edward G. Hoseah: "Article, Corruption as a global hindrance to promoting ethics, integrity, and sustainable development in Tanzania: the role of the anti-corruption agency" published online: 4th November, 2014, https://www.tandfonline.com/doi/full/10.1080/17449626.2014.973995 (Edward G. Hoseah is the Director General of Prevention and Combating of Corruption Board in Tanzania and is a member of the Tanzania Bar Association. He was the first President of the Eastern Africa Association of Anti-Corruption Authorities. He also served as a Chairman of the Southern African Forum Against Corruption and the African Union Advisory Boar on Corruption. he is currently Vice President of International Association of Anti Corruption Authorties and is also a Board member of the International Society for the Reform of Criminal Law.)
2. Misra, R.K. (1957). *Political Legacy of Plato and Aristotle*; Allahabad: Kitab Mahal.
3. Das, Das. "Environmental Ethics Matter to Philosophy?" In "*Manavayatam*", Vol. II. No. II, January–June 2013.
4. Chapter 2, Democratic Governance for Human Development; Human Development Report 2002, published for the United Nations Development Programme (UNDP), New York, Oxford; Oxford University Press 2002).
5. Lawton, Alan and Michael Macaulay (2009); "Ethics Management and Ethical Management"; In *Ethics and Integrity in Public Administration, Concepts and Cases*; edited by Raymond W. Cox III, M.E. Sharpe, Inc.
6. Goel, Aruna and S.L. Goel (2005). *Human Values and Education*, Published by Deep & Deep Publications Pvt. Ltd., New Delhi.
7. World Medical Association' Medical Ethics Manual BP.63.01212 Femey-Voltaire Cedex, France. website. www wma.net)
8. Donald Treadwell, Donald and Jill B. Treadwell (2005). *Public Relations Writing*; Second Edition; Response Books; A Division of Sage Publications, New Delhi.
9. R.K. Misra, R.K.: *Ibid.*
10. Rao, V.V. (1980). *History of Political Thought*, New Delhi: S. Chand & Company.
11. Robertson, Ian: (1980). *Sociology*, Worth Publishers, Inc. New York.
12. World Commission on Culture and Development 1995; UN200a: *Globalization and Cultural Choice*; chapter 5, Box 5:2 Human Development Report 2004, (published for UNDP).
13. Ebadi, Shirin. (2004) *Globalization and Cultural Choice*; chapter 5, Human Development Report 2004; UNDP.
14. Tiwari, Kedarnath, *Comparative Religion*, Motilal Banarasi Dass: Delhi.
15. Radhakrishnan (1970). *The Present Crisis of Faith*, Delhi: Orient.

16. Baxi (1994). *Human Rights and Human Wrongs*, New Delhi: Har Anand Publications.
17 Sharma, G. (1998). *Human Rights and Legal Remedies*; New Delhi: Deep and Deep Publication.
18. en.wikipedia.org/wiki/Human Rights.
19. www.ohchr.org/en/issues/pages/whatarehuman rights.aspx
20. Naseema, C.: (2002). *Human Rights; Human Rights Education: Conceptual and Pedagological Aspects*, New Delhi: Kanishka Publisher Distributors.
21. Aung San Suu Kyi, winer of Nobel Peace Prize, (1991), Human Development Report 2002, page, 51, box 2.1, published for the United Nations development programme (UNDP) New York, Oxford, Oxford University Press, 2002.
22. Sharma, Gakuleh (2000). *Ibid.*
23. www.ohchr.org/en/issues/pages/whatarehuman rights.aspx
24. Canely and Jones: (1945) Canley, Simon and Peter Jones (ed) (1945): *Human Rights and Global Diversity*: by Frank Cass: London.
25. UNESCO: 1978.
26. Kofi Annan (2002). United Nations Development Programme (UNDP) New York, Oxford: Oxford University Press.
27. Tripathi, Anil. "Gandhiji's Social Philosophy", in *Journal of Gandhian Stidies*, Vol. 7, No. 28, July 1980, Gandhi Bhawan, University of Allahabad, Allahabad.
28. (Quartey) Quartey, Francis Ofosu: "Gandhian Concept of Non-violence": in *Journal of Gandhian Stidies*, Vol. 7 No. 28 July, 1980, Gandhi Bhawan, University of Allahabad, Allahabad.
29. Verma, Dr. Surendra. (1978) *Modern Search for Peace*, in *Journal of Gandhian Studies*: Vol. 5 No. 21, October 1978.
30. Quartey Francis Ofosu. "Gandhian Concept of Non-violence", in *Journal of Gandhian Studies*, Vol. 7. No. 28, July 1980, Gandhi Bhawan, University of Allahabad, Allahabad.
31. Tripathi, Anil. "Gandhiji's Social Philosophy", In *Journal of Gandhian Stidies*, Vol. 7 No. 28, July 1980 Gandhi Bhawan, University of Allahabad, Allahabad.
32. Tripathi, Anil. "Gandhiji's Social Philosophy", In *Journal of Gandhian Stidies* Vol. 7 No. 28 July 1980 Gandhi Bhawan, University of Allahabad, Allahabad.
33. Publication of Department of Information and Public Relations, 26.12.2010, Vol. XXXI, No. I.
34. *Young India*: 7.5.1931. Gandhi: *Young India*; 13th November, 1924.
35. Mahatma: *Harijan*, 5th May 1946.
36. K. Munirathnam: (1987) "Relevance of Gandhian Conception of Freedom to Present Society: in *Journal of Gandhian Studies*; Vol. 14, No. 54-55; January-April, Institute of Gandhian Thought & Peace Studies; Gandhi Bhawan; University of Allahabad, Allahabad.

37. Radhakrishnan (1992). *The Present Crisis of Faith*, Orient Papaerback books, 11th ed.
38. Palkhivala (1997).
39. Bakshi, P.M. (2004). *The Constitution of India*, Delhi: Universal Law Publishing Company, Fifth edition.
40. Agarwal, (1986). *Constitutional Development of India and National Movement*, S. Chand and Co., Delhi.
41. Adams Guy and Danny, L. Balfour (1984). "Ethical Failing, Incompetence and Administrative Evil (Lessons from Kartina and Iraq", In *Ethics and Integrity in Public Administration: Concepts and Cases*; Edited by Raymond W. Cox III, New York: M.E. Sharpe.
42. Bharatiya, L.K. (1987). "Prospect of Change in Gandhian Lines", *Journal of Gandhian Studies*, Gandhi Bhawan, University of Allahabad, Allahabad.
43. Mohnot, S.R. (2007). Relevance of Hindu Philosophy to Understand India, In *Understanding India* edited by Subhash Chandra Kashyap and Abhaya Kashayap, New Delhi: Vitasta Pubishing Ltd.
44. Radhakrishnan (1970).
45. V.R. Krishna Iyer (1980). *Justice and Beyond*, Deep & Deep Publications; Rajouri Garden, New Delhi, 110027.
46. Human Rights teaching, file:/A/Node002/network%209famyo/human%20Rights%20t Teaching htm.26.5
47. Radhakrishnan, S. (1961). *Recovery of Faith*, by George Allen and Unwin Ltd.
48. Hazarika, N. (2012). "Ethical Vacuity in Administration" In *Democratic Administration for Good Governance*.
49. Mukhopadhyay, Lipi (2002). Social Conditioning and Deviant Behaviour, IIPJ, Spl. No. Social Tensions; July-September, Vol. XLVIII, No. 3.
50. Doctor, Adi (1997). *Political Thinkers of Modern India*, New Delhi: Mittal Publications.

VI
Gandhian Way to Eradicate Corruption

Mahatma Gandhi epitomizes the concept of a human being through his lifestyle and activities. The message of truth, non-violence and human rights which he left for the global human society will always remain relevant in the world. His socio-political ideas help us to regenerate the contemporary world to make it a place where one can think of a peaceful human life. Apparently, Gandhi's altruistic philosophy may be viewed as unrealistic or utopian in the world of today, but deep understanding of it provides enough scope to realize that it is the best alternative solution to most of our problems. And it is the only way to lead a healthy social life beginning from the family to the global society. The speeches of the world leaders like Kofi Anan, Antonio Guteress Nelson Mandela, Shirin Ebadi etc. the resolutions of UNO and the world conferences on social, political and economic issues help us not only to appreciate Gandhi's ideas but also to realize that his philosophy is one of the best devices to save the world from the scourge of serious ailments of the world community and corruption is not an exception to it. His altruistic philosophy and idea of *Sarvodaya* are echoed in the policies like 'Health for All', 'Sports for All', 'Education for All' etc. The nations of the modern world cannot afford to reject Gandhi's philosophy as an utopian hope. Because human rights and human dignity are the means and end of a human society. Here I will discuss Non-violence, Truth and Sarvodaya in the context of Corruption in administration.

Coming to India, one cannot deny the progress of science and technology, education, standard of living and several reforms in the socio-economic and political life of the Indians. In almost every front of public services noticeable changes have taken place. Simultaneously, however, corruption, violation of human rights, hypocrisy, unethical activities, severe frailness of human power to control violent activism of money and muscle power, lack of serious thought to the consequences of the politicization of public services, buying and selling of job, massive growth of fake financial and educational institutions exploiting the poor and innocent Indians' hard earned money and helpless unemployed youths by all possible means may be considered as a serious threat to the nation. Under this situation Gandhi's ideas, I feel, will certainly help to a great extent to relieve the nation from various kinds of ailment.

On 15th June, 2007 the UNO decided to observe the International Day of Non-Violence each year on 2nd October, 2007 – the birth anniversary of Mahatma Gandhi, who helped lead India to independence and inspired movements for civil rights and freedom across the world.

Introducing the resolution adopted by 192-member body, Anand Sharma, India's Minister of State for External Relations said the idea originated at an international conference on "Peace, Non-Violence and Empowerment – Gandhian Philosophy in the 21st century" convened in New Delhi in January in 2007. He also pointed out that Gandhi's 'novel mode of mass mobilization and non-violent action' inspired leaders like Nelson Mandela, Martin Luther King Jr. etc.[1]

The nations of the world have experienced the worst consequences of wars – heavy loss of man and material. Even wars that were fought for a good cause, like the Civil War of the United States of America, that resulted in slavery being abolished, have been responsible for many deaths.[2]

Referring to International Day of Non-Violence, UN Secretary-General Antonio Guterres said, "Gandhi proved that non-violence can change history. Let us be inspired by his courage and conviction as we continue our work to advance peace, sustainable development and human rights for all of the peoples of the world." This International Day is an occasion to "disseminate the message of non-violence, including through education and public awareness." The UN resolution reaffirms, "the universal relevance of the principle of non-violence" and "the desire to secure a culture of peace, tolerance, understanding and non-violence."[3]

The International Day of Non-Violence is celebrated every year on 2nd October throughout the world on birth anniversary of Mahatma Gandhi, leader of Indian Independence Movement and also pioneer of philosophy of non-violence, i.e. *Ahimsa*.

Gandhi is well known for his great contribution to the struggle of Indians to make the country free from clutches of British. He was born on 2nd October, 1869 in Porbandar, in Bombay Presidency of British India.

He is fondly known as "Bapu" for his selfless contribution towards India's Independence Movement. He is also called as Father of the Nation.[4]

Martin Luther King Jr. said, "Non-violence means avoiding not only external physical violence but also internal violence of spirit. You not only refuse to shoot a man, but also refuse to hate him."

Non-violence is both a principle and a practice. The principle of non-violence affirms the active use of non-coercive and non-aggressive means to create a peaceful context. It is based on the assumption that justice will eventually prevail, that choices should be made from a place of love rather than hate, that the hurtful action, not the person, should be subdued and that voluntary suffering has value as an important facet of life.

In practice, non-violence involves actively peaceful behaviour in the midst of conflict. With the help of non-violent means we can reduce our irrational elements. During Twentieth century, the successful social movements of Gandhi in India and Martin Luther King Jr. in the United States led to the people's realization of completely new dimensions of non-violence.[5]

Professor Gene Sharp, a leading scholar on Non-violent resistance, defined non-violence, in his publication, 'The Politics of Non-violent Action' as, "Non-violent action is a technique by which people who reject passivity and submission, and who see struggle as essential, can wage their conflict without violence. Non-violent action is not an attempt to avoid or ignore conflict. It is a response to the problem of how to act effectively in politics, especially how to wield powers effectively." One key tenet of the theory of non-violence is that the power of rulers depends on the consent of the people, and non-violence therefore, seeks to undermine such power through withdrawal of the consent and cooperation of the populace. There are three main categories of non-violent action:

- Protest and persuasion, including marches and vigils;
- Non-cooperation; and
- Non-violent intervention, such as blockades and occupations.[6]

Mahatma Gandhi believed that the problems of life can be dealt with the help of non-violence. It is a technique of resistance to injustice that would not lead to fresh exploitation or violence. It may also be used as the basic principle for social and economic development.

Non-violent resistance is a peaceful and democratic means of social and political change. To him love and persuasion should be the means of change not hatred.

Reason, peace, democracy and non-violence go together. Peace is meaningless without non-violence; democracy is impossible without non-violence; and reason cannot function without non-violence and democracy. Ultimately, reason must conquer the destructive urges on will to power, will to rule and will to dominate. The crude law of the jungle must be replaced by the law of love and non-violence, if humanity is to evolve further. To him resistance to evil is a duty it is not a method, it is quality of mind.[7]

Mahatma Gandhi conceived the idea of *Satyagraha* as a weapon during the struggle launched by the Indians in South Africa against racial discrimination made by the white minority. This was sharpened during the non-cooperation and civil disobedience movements against the British Government in India.

Gandhi defined *Satyagraha* as the 'soul force'. This concept rejects violence and hatred in all forms. It is a search for truth without involving the opponent. *Satyagraha* underlines four basic elements – (1) use of soul force; (2) exclusion of physical force; (3) it is an appeal to convert the wrong doer; and (4) both means and end are convertible terms. This force may be used by individuals as well as by communities. It may be used against any kind of oppression or exploitation. It has universal nature.

Satyagrahi has confidence on the power of spirit, truth, love by which he can overcome evil through self-suffering and self-sacrifice. It is a Gandhian technique to fight against evil.

Satyagraha has different forms. The most familiar forms are non-cooperation and civil disobedience. Non-cooperation includes strike, hartal, boycott, resignation of offices and titles etc. Civil Disobedience is a form of non-violent rebellion. By refusing to obey the 'immoral laws' of the state, the civil resister denies the existence of the established authority. In doing so he never uses force.

Satyagraha is a method, Gandhi used to fight against evil and injustice. The significance of this method is that it can be used by all individuals and communities without dishonouring human values. This method tells the rulers or the authority that obedience to law is not automatic. It must have the capacity to secure support of the people. A true *Satyagrahi* tries to eliminate the gaps between theory and practice or word and work of the policy makers.

Once a government becomes autocratic and corrupt, violent and unjust, it does not listen to the common citizens, to Gandhi, the citizens have the right to withdraw their cooperation with the regime. Disloyalty to such a regime becomes a duty and disobedience a virtue. However, Gandhi's concept of *Satyagraha* as an instrument to bring change in the regime was not free from criticism. The persons like M.N. Roy, Rajendra Prasad, B.R. Ambedkar etc. had doubt on the strength of this weapon to be used effectively in all situations brought by social changes.[8]

Truth for Gandhi is knowledge. It is the full awareness of one's being in any situation. This awareness makes a man happy irrespective of the situation to which he belongs. To Gandhi where there is truth, there is knowledge which is true and therefore, knowledge is associated with God. Gandhi's truth is the main principle of governing a man's life. This principle can make a man free from confusion that arises from conflict and widens the path for taking best decision in the conflicting situation. Under such a situation things work out in a systematic manner and provides scope for authentic unity. Gandhi was in search of truth which will elevate the social relationship to a higher level. Apparently, the ethical principles of different religions may be different, but ultimately, all religions move towards the principle of respecting the human dignity. In other words every religion is based on morality. Gandhi did not make any effort to promote moral uniformity, but to an honest commitment to the truth.[9]

Gandhi said morality addresses certain qualities of the individuals, such as, nobleness of character, purity of soul and motive, notion of truth, selfless service and goodness of means. Full development of human personality is based on morality. The peaceful social order is possible when all individuals work or move together with understanding of human values.[10]

Truth is a significant aspect of Gandhi's social philosophy. The pursuit of truth does not admit violence being inflicted on one's own opponent. The adversary is opponent, not enemy, and he is to be won by patience and sympathy. And patience means self-suffering which comes to mean "vindication of truth not by infliction of suffering on the opponent but on one's self". Gandhi understood suffering to be neither negative nor a necessary evil. Rather he understood it to be a positive force in its own right, and even more powerful instrument than violence. "Real suffering bravely borne melts even a heart of stone. Such is the potency of suffering and *tapas*. And there lies key to *Satyagraha*. As against it, violence is intended to achieve an end through the exploitation of fear. It strengthens the elements of passion and compulsion. But suffering appeals to a man's moral nature. It brings out the elements of love and compassion. It was Gandhi's firm conviction that "human nature in its essence is one and therefore unfailingly responds to the advances of love". And success is the certain result of suffering of the extremist character, voluntarily undergone."[11]

To Gandhi *Ahimsa* and Truth are so intertwined that it is difficult to disentangle and separate them. They are like the two sides of a coin or rather of a smooth unstamped metalic disc. *Ahimsa* is the means and Truth is the end. Gandhi's definition of *Ahimsa* is very wide. He said every act of giving pain to the mind or body of any living creature directly or indirectly is, in his view is a breach of *Ahimsa*. Hence harsh words. Harsh judgements, ill-will, anger and spite, lust and cruelty should be viewed as insidious forms of *Himsa*. And slow torture of men and animals, the starvation and exploitation to which they are subjected out of selfish greed, wanton humiliation and suppression of the weak and the killing of their self-respect that we witness all around us – there is *Himsa* in them. In short Gandhi's doctrine of non-violence is nothing but Law of Love preached by all the saints of the world as the law of life.

Gandhi wished spreading of the message of non-violence from individuals to nations and inventing technique for its application. When nations as well as individuals learn to give up violence which is the mark of the brute, his teaching will be looked upon as a landmark in the history of humanity and he will be recognized as a benefactor of the species. His message is, therefore, not limited to India or to Indians. It is addressed to the whole world and to the entire race of man. Indian politics was the only platform from which he delivered his message, which is is really universal. He wrote, "I believe my message to be universal, but as yet I feel that I can show visible success in India, the delivery of the message becomes complete."[12]

To get rid of the problem of corruption, which is a psychological disease of a man human approach is the right and strong device to be used even in the modern world of today. This approach requires creation of a favourable environment at home and society so that a child can develop the habits of behaving in such direction. Educational institution must also try to educate the students in a situation where the principles of truth and non-violence can influence them. These can easily be reflected in the teacher student relationship, lifestyle and functioning of the teachers, examination systems, honour of human rights and human dignity etc. The role of the family and other social institutions is very significant in this context. Because every service provider reaches to that status after passing through the stages of the process from being to becoming. During childhood and youth hood he/she learns many things through socializing process in which family and educational institutions play a significant role as primary agents. What he or she learns from these social institutions, mainly from the parents and family community environment and social values are reflected in his or her attitude and behaviour as service provider to the society. The attitude and behaviour of the service providers are very deeply rooted in the social and family culture. Significantly, they are also influenced by the changing social values and culture. The appearance of corruption, unethical activities, inhuman treatment etc. in the services are found mainly due to several sociological factors like these, besides other factors. Failure of the socializing agencies in achieving their goals brings failure of human power to control other external powers and an individual in this situation may become the slave of any destructive power or activities. They start losing the reasoning power. Here begins the self-abasement as human being. From whichever direction wind comes they will be blown easily because they cannot be firm on their feet as they have lost the human power. They forget their identity as human being and allow animal power to function. Gandhi's approach can make a man internally strong to make a man in a right direction.

Gandhi said, "My daily experience, as those who are working with me, is that every problem would lend itself to solution if we are determined to make the law of truth and non-violence the law of life. For truth and non-violence are, to me two faces of the same coin."[13]

Like truth non-violence is also a social instrument to fight against social evils. Non-violent approach demands that the adherents must possess positive values of courage, absence of ill will against its adversary, self-control and self-abnegation.[14]

Gandhi views non-violence in terms of thought, word and deed. It is positive love even to evil doer. Non-violence is the basic foundation of *Satyagraha* and is a weapon of the strong. It requires enormous discipline and training in non-violent actions. It does not depend on physical force, but on moral force. It is not a new ideal it is rooted in the Indian culture and tradition.

Gene Sharp said the *Satyagrahi* seeks to improve his own life to combat social evils by non-violent action and build a better social order by constructive work. To adhere to and train oneself in non-violent action is not merely rational decision, but a moral duty for mankind today to ensure peace in every walk of life. The basic principles of *Satyagraha* are:

- Non-violence trough self-suffering.
- Ends and means: only non-violent and peaceful means can achieve truthful ends.
- Faith in goodness of human nature.

To be a *Satyagrahi* one must have certain qualities according to R.B. Gregg, such as – habits of obedience, self-respect and self-reliance, self-control and self-sacrifice, tenacity of will, sense of unity with fellow members, energy, courage etc. Further he suggests the principles of truth, love, spiritual unity, equality, gentleness, simplicity, self-purification and self-suffering as means of persuasion. Satyagraha and non-violence are the two basic instruments used by Gandhi for resolving almost all social or human problems. These two weapons are also relevant to eradicate the problem of corruption in the modern world.[15]

In addition to these Gandhi's concept of *Sarvodaya* based on the scheme of Village *Swaraj* helps to understand the concept of Good Governance which is occupying a key position in the discussion on good governance among the scholars, politicians, administrators and reformers. Good governance is also a device with universal nature to remove unethical behaviour of the administrators in a democratic country.

Gandhi's ideal society is based on the power of non-violence, love, and 'good of all' or *Sarvodaya*.[16]

While criticizing western materialism, Gandhi said, "our young men who have received western education are full of spirit. This spirit should be directed into the right channels, as otherwise it can only do us harm". *Swaraj* really means self-control. Only he is capable of self-control who observes the rules of morality, does not cheat or give up truth, and does his duty to his parents, wife and children, servants and neighbours. Such a man is in enjoyment of *Swaraj*, no matter where he lives.

Gandhi visulalized a new India which would attain *Swaraj* through "righteous methods", i.e. "our *Swaraj* must be real *Swaraj*, which cannot be atained by either violence or industrialization". Truth is for Gandhi the philosopher's stone, which alone could effect this kind of transformation.[17]

He defines *Swadeshi* "as the spirit in us which restricts us to the use and service of our immediate surroundings." It is a first step in self-sacrifice, it is the love of one's neighbour, it is an effective social service, it is a form of non-violence. It is *Swadharma* applied to one's immediate environment.[18]

In a Research Monograph prepared by Dr. S.L. Melhorta and Dr. S.K. Sharma on 'Village Reconstruction: Gandhian Way' highlighted two major objectives of Gandhi's scheme of Village Reconstruction—one was the eradication of economic ills and the other one was reconstruction of rural society based on certain human values of truth and non-violence, love, co-operation etc. These constituted the essence of Gandhi's way of Life. It is a view of civilization that assures to all individuals, freedom, and enduring peace, full development of all their faculties, healthy environment and harmonious relations with their fellow members. This plan involves rebuilding of every aspect of human life—social, political and economic. It envisages a society based on self-supporting and self-governing villages. But it does not aim at the resurections of old village life vitiated by sufferings superstitions and obsolete customs but the formation of small independent and self-reliant communities settled in villages where life is simple and pure, where all enjoy social, political and economic freedom as a result of mutual cooperation and hard work.

In terms of politics it is nearest to his concept of a stateless society, for, there is minimum control from above since the individuals are themselves involved in the making and implementation of the decisions concerning the administration of the village. Gandhi depicted the village administration as, "*Swaraj* is a complete republic, independent of its neighbours for its own vital wants, and yet interdependent for many others in which dependence is a necessity. Thus, every village's first concern will be to grow its own food crops and cotton for its cloth. It should have a reserve for its own cattle, recreation and playground for adults and children. Then, if there is more land available, it will grow useful money crops, thus excluding *ganja*, tobacco, opium and the like. The village will maintain a village theatre, school and public hall. It will have its own water works ensuring clean water supply.... Education will be compulsory up to the final basic course. As far as possible every activity will be conducted on the cooperative basis. There will be no caste such as we have today with their graded untouchability. Non-violence with its technique of *Satyagraha* and non-co-operation will be the sanction of the village community There will be a compulsory service of the village guards who will be selected by rotation from the register maintained by the village. The government of the village will be conducted by the Panchayat of five persons annually elected by the adult villagers, male and female, possessing minimum qualifications.... This Panchayat will be the legislature, judiciary and executive."

A village will be like a family. The Hindus, the Muslims, the Sikhs, the Parsees and the Christians live as brothers and sisters. There is hardly any trace of untouchability in the community. It means that there would be no separate quarters for Harijans. It follows that the members of this community must have high character. It is a highly cultured society in which every man and woman knows what he or she wants and what is more, knows that no one should want anything that others cannot have with equal labour. In Gandhi's view this kind of society must be based on truth and non-violence.

Village sanitation was of main consideration in Gandhi's scheme of rural reconstruction. He recommended simple, inexpensive and effective remedies for tackling the problem of village insanitation. These aimed not only to keep the surroundings clean but also sought to convert the dirt into a source of wealth. He also suggested certain ways of disposing of refuse. These can be buried for two purposes— for promotion of villagers' health and for production of manure. Emphasis on hygiene is the first consideration in the village reconstruction scheme of Gandhi.

He looked upon supply of pure water to villagers as of glorious service with incalculable benefit to the suffering humanity of India, since its neglect was responsible for many of the diseases suffered by villagers. To him nature is the first physician, which is continuously repairing what man has damaged.

He believed that where the rules of personnel, domestic and public sanitation are strictly observed and due care is taken in the matter of diet and exercise; there would be no scope for illness or disease.

Nature cure was a part of his plan of self-reliant society. It depends on right and balanced diet. So to produce enough vegetables, fruits and milk in the villages is an essential part of nature cure. It most suitable in villages because it does not depend upon costly equipment.

Self-sufficiency is the keynote of the economy of this society. It means that all the requirements in the way of food and other necessities of life will be grown or manufactured in the village. Only thing is that the people have to adjust their taste for the production of basic food or raw material such as cotton for the cottage industry. Sericulture and cottage industry are the foundations of its economic structure. He says, "In India the problem with us is not how to find leisure for the teaming millions inhabiting our villages. The problem is that how to utilize their idle hours, which are equal to the working days of six months in the year...." Gandhi had no objection to villagers in using modern machines and tools provided they are not "used as a means of exploitation of others. One has to be very careful in the use of modern machines in the villages. The most important industries which can be easily started in any village are *khadi*, hand-grinding, hand-pounding, soap-making, papermaking, match-making, oil-pressing etc. He wanted the villagers to develop such a high degree of skill that articles prepared by them should command a ready market outside. All this could not be achieved without proper education which must cater to the real needs of the villagers.

In pursuit of ideal of village self-sufficiency, he advocated reliance on village industries. This, in his opinion, would give employment to the millions of villagers who were living in idleness.

Referring to Panchayat system, Gandhi said democracy cannot be realized without Panchayat working as the basic and effective unit of government since true democracy in his view, cannot be worked by twenty men sitting at the centre. It has to be worked from below by the people of every village. He was confident that the will of the people would assert itself through the effective working of the Panchayat. The public opinion will do what violence can never do. The functions of the Panchayat cover every aspect of life of the village community since its task is to transform a village from a dung heap to a tiny garden of Eden where dwell highly intelligent folk whom no one can deceive or exploit.

While talking about self-sufficient and self governing villages, he emphasized that the village will not work in isolation. He envisaged a structure of government for the country based on autonomous villages that cooperate with each other in making human life happier and richer. So he argued, "In this structure composed of innumerable villages, there will be ever widening, never ascending circles. Life will not be a pyramid with apex sustained by the bottom. But it will be a circle whose centre will be the individual always ready to perish for the village, never aggressive in their arrogance but ever humble, sharing the majesty of the circle of which they are integrated units.[19]

Gandhi's Village Swaraj and Sarvodaya reflects the the essentials of good governance in a rudimentary form. Good governance is a strong device to eradicate corruption. Gandhi may be considered as as an architect of it. Good governance is nothing but democratic governance with moral dimension.

To Gandhi democracy is a way of life. Today the word Democracy has become a common word used by the citizens of a modern state. They have enough faith in the democratic principles. But experience in India shows that in reality average people do not practice them in their lives though they have faith in them and express the need of these principles in public speeches and writings. Adherence of democratic principles or to follow a democratic way of life is not an easy task, it requires perseverance, mental strength and commitment to the cause of humanity. It is also a difficult task as the whole concept of democracy centres round human being and success of democracy depends on activism of human power along with other qualities.

The freedom struggle under the leadership of Mahatma Gandhi may be called as the struggle for democratic way of life in all fields of man's life—political, social, economic, legal, religious—both within and outside the family—public or private. After gaining independence the framers of the Constitution of India took utmost care to see that it would provide a wide path on which all Indians, irrespective of caste, creed, place of birth, sex etc. can travel without difficulty to reach the destination of establishing a democratic society in India. But, the human power of commitment to the efforts of the framers of the Constitution and the freedom fighters could not be sustained by both the rulers and the ruled in independent India. Nani A. Palkhiwala, an eminent personality in the field of law, pointed out four costly failures of the government and the people which are the direct causes of it as below:

1. Failure to maintain law and order. We have too much government and too little administration: too many public servants and too little public service; too many controls and too little welfare; too many laws and too many justice;
2. Failure to bring the unbounded economic potential of the country to fruition;
3. Failure to make human investment—investment in education, family planning, nutrition and public health, in contradiction to physical investment in factories and plants. Gross national happiness; and
4. Failure to provide moral leadership.[20]

The responsibility for this state of affairs must be shared by both the rulers and the ruled. While discussing this issue we have to underline the state as the largest component of the Indian governance. The Leading personalities in the fields of politics, administration, education, social work, religions constitute very significant component of the Indian governance. They are the role models for the rest of the society. Unfortunately, experience shows that most of them maintain multi standards of life which is not easily understandable by the common men. They hide their inner motive very skilfully while approaching the general masses for participation in their programmes. They have become slaves of money and move as directed by money power. Naturally, they lose the capacity to judge what is good and what is bad even for their own lives. Criminalization of politics is a serious ailment in Indian democracy affecting the human rights of the people at every walk of life. The administration is not responsive, responsible and accountable to the public even for genuine causes. The common people are exploited and cheated by falsehood and dishonesty in various forms. As mentioned above it is not because of lack of laws or rules and regulations and institutions to safeguard human rights of different sections of the people. What is lacking is the obedience to human values and human dignity. Today priority is given to accumulation of money by any means and any amount without limitation and building of huge property—movable or immovable at the cost of human rights of our own people. Now the question before us is how to save the human beings from this new form of slavery caused by the money and muscle power in modern India. Disraeli said, "Money is not the measure of a man, but it is often the means of finding out how small he is." It is difficult no doubt but not impossible to redirect the society towards humanity so that each individual can be released from uncomfortable stay in the domain of monetary slavery.

Nani A. Palkhiwala rightly said, "In a vast democracy like India, many citizens are bound to be undimensional. But no lawyer has any excuse for being undimensional. By his training and equipment and by his professional competence he is better qualified than the rest of the citizenry to take an active part in the making of laws and the formulation of public policies. He would be failing to serve his country if he did not do this duty." This is applicable to every public service provider. Today ethical vacuum in every walk of life is causing deviation from the real path of human progress.

Acharya J.B. Kripalani spoke in the Constituent Assembly on 17th October, 1949, "I want this House to remember that what we have enunciated are not merely legal, constitutional and formal principles, but moral principles; and moral principles have to be lived in life. They have to be lived, whether it is in private life, or it is in public life, whether it is in commercial life, political life of an administrator. They have to be lived throughout." But very soon these principles are withering away.

The concept of democracy cannot be understood fully without reference to human rights. The journey of a man from the status of cave-man who was exposed to all kinds of natural calamities and attacks of wild animals to that of democratic man, who is safeguarded on every aspect of his life was piloted by faith in human rights and dignity. During this period man had to struggle against the violent forces of nature and wild animals in every walk of life. This journey will always remind us that human rights are not created in thin air. These are the results of untiring and long struggle of man for survival. In course of journey man has realized the dignity of human being. And explicit expression of it is found in the emergence of the concept of democracy.[21]

Priority of duties is referred to in *smritis*. The eleventh chapter of *Gautama Smriti*, a King is considered not fit to levy taxes on the citizens if he does not perform his duties faithfully, diligently and consciously. G.S. Misra, in his article, *Limits of Statutory Rights* said, "Moral conduct and obligation to discharge one's duties was considered essential for both king and the people. The spirit of devotion to duty was, therefore, instilled in all the citizens in various ways. It was done not only through education but also by making it an integral aspect of the traditional value system which were absorbed even while one was growing up. A society which was built upon such foundations inherently guaranteed the human rights. These were the very notions which made India a land of true action or *Karma Bhumi*."

During freedom struggle Gandhi also stated in support of the above tradition of the country that true source of right is duty. The framers of the Constitution have provided enough scope for its realization. The human rights cannot be enjoyed by an individual without human duties. In other words, these are not absolute in nature. The limitation originates from the fact that each human being has similar rights.[22]

But in independent India neither the rulers nor the ruled honoured this Indian tradition. They have started giving weight age to rights only. Negligence of duty has become the law of the average people. The political leaders have become more concern of the security of their political positions, nation's interest has been neglected to a great extent.

Gandhi started struggle for human rights in South Africa and later in India. He pointed out another significant feature of social life. Gandhiji bridged the gap between individual and social ethics and regarded social reality as a counterpart of man's inner reality. To him individual freedom had a value but one must not, he said, "forget that man is essentially a social being. He has risen to present status by learning to adjust his individualism to the requirements of social progress." [23]

To Gandhi there must be non-violence in the private life itself. He lived in an atmosphere of non-violence from the Jainism of non-violence, his saintly mother, disciplined father and tolerant wife. It gave him a scope to learn and practice the principles of non-violence and truth.

Gandhi also emphasized the need of moral leadership who will be the soul of mass Satyagraha. The most important qualities of the leader are:

(a) Sincerity and all-embracing love;
(b) Culture and dignified bearing;
(c) Self-control;
(d) Selflessness;
(e) Pursuit of non-possession;
(f) Rooted in the soil of and having the spirit of *Swadeshi;*
(g) Faith in God which is synonymous with truth should be unshakable.[24]
(h) To be a true servant of the human being he must be the possessor of above qualities. Because these qualities make a man human. Human society can be served effectively only by a human being not by a half- human being or by an animal, just as only the democrats can make democratic way of life successful.[25]

Today's socio-political situation in India induces a researcher or a social scientist to think that the way of life of an Indian has to be grounded in the Indian tradition and philosophy to make the country strong and suitable for living with human dignity. While adjusting with the changes in the modern world he must be well acquainted with the Indian tradition and philosophy to serve the country successfully. Mere expertness or knowledge on a particular issue or modern equipment are not enough unless the user of these is selfless, moral and sympathetic to the people. The author makes an attempt to bring to light the relevance of Gandhian way to eradicate social ailments in contemporary India.

It may be noted that at a time when many people in Ghana and Africa had a doubt about the need of study of the philosophy of Non-violence as advocated by Gandhi Francis Ofosu Quartey, Secretary of Gandhi Brotherhood League, Ghana expressed his personal feeling that it was necessary for the following reasons:

1. "It is the most original contribution of India to political thought and practice;
2. *Satyagraha* was the lifelong study and practice of Gandhi. To know Gandhi one must know what *Satyagraha* is;
3. *Satyagraha* formed the philosophical background of the struggle of India for independence. To understand the meaning of the struggle and present institutions of India one must know the meaning and the body of ideas which constitute *Satyagraha*."[26]

The evolution of *Satyagraha* by Mahatma Gandhi has made him the most significant figure in the world. Non-violence in social life is not peculiar to Indian people. History is replete with leaders who have advocated non-violence. However, India is unique in having a tradition of non-violence and it is India's greatest contribution to the world.

REFERENCES

1. https://news.un.org/en./story/2007/06/222502-un-declares-2-october-gandhis-birthday-international-day-non-violence accessed 0n 25th March, 2019.
2. https://www.daysoftheyear.com/days/international-day-of-non-violence accessed on 25th March 2019

3. http://www.un.org/events/non-violenceday/ accessed 25th March, 2019.
4. https://currentaffairs.gktoday.intags/international-day-of-non-vilence, accessed on 25th March, 2019.
5. https://internatinal day of peace.org/get-involved/nonviolence/ accessed on 25th March, 2019.
6. https://www.un.org/en/events/nonviolenceday/background.shtml accessed on 25th March, 2019.
7. Rao, K.L. Seshagiri; (1978) "Non-Violence and Peace;" in the *Journal of Gandhian Studies*: Vol. 3 No. 21, October 1978; University of Allahabad.
8. Dilip K. Chatterjee; (1979) Relevance of Satyagraha as a Technique of Conflict Resolution, in the *Journal of Gandhian Studies*, April 1979 Vol. 6. No. 23.
9. Collected Works of Mahatma Gandhi, Vol. 23. Government of India Publication.
10. Kh. Budhachandra Singh, Unpublished Ph.D. thesis on Gandhian Approach to Non-Violence and Peace, submitred to Manipur University, 2011.
11. Grover, Dr. D.C.: Satyagraha: (1977) *An Answer to International Conflict; Institute of Gandhian Thought and Peace*; Gandhi Bhawan; University of Allahabad; Vol. 4 No. 16. July 1977.
12. Sarma, D.S. (1967). *Hinduism Through The Ages:* Bharatiya Vidya Bhawan; Chowpatty; Bombay.
13. Ashok Singh. (1984) "Power of Non-Violence: Gandhian Concept", In the *Journal of Gandhian Studies*, Institute of Gandhian Thought and Peace Studies, Gandhi Bhawan; University of Allahabad; Vol. 11. No. 43-44, April/July 1984.
14. Kh. Budhachandra Singh, Unpublished Ph.D. thesis, submitted to Manipur University, 2011.
15. *Young India*, First October, 1931.
16. Ashok Singh. "Power of Non-Violence: Gandhian Concept", In the *Journal of Gandhian Studies*, Institute of Gandhian Thought and Peace Studies, Gandhi Bhawan; University of Allahabad; Vol. 11. No. 43-44, April/July 1984.
17. Detlef Kantowsky, University of Konstanz, Germany (West) paper contributed to: "Modern Search for Peace: The Gandhian Way" conference of the Indian Society of Gandhian Studies.
18. Sarma, D.S. (1967). *Hinduism Through The Ages:* Chowpatty; Bombay: Bharatiya Vidya Bhawan.
19. Malhorta, Dr. S.L. and Dr. S.K. Sharma; Research Monograph; Towards Village Swaraj, January 1977; Department of Gandhian Studies, Panjab University; Chandigarh.
20. Palkhiwala, Nani A: (1997) *We The People*; UBS Publisher' Distributors Ltd. New Delhi, 11th print.

21. *Palkhiwala* 1997: *Ibid.*
22. Baxi (994). *Human Rights and Human Wrongs*, New Delhi: Har Anand Publications.
23. Tripathi, Anil (1980). "Gandhiji's Social Philosophy", In *Journal of Gandhian Stidies*, Vol. 7 No. 28 July 1980 Gandhi Bhawan, University of Allahabad – Allahabad.
24. Quartey, Francis Ofosu. (1980) "Gandhian Concept of Non-violence", In *Journal of Gandhian Studies*, Vol. 7 No. 28 July, Gandhi Bhawan, University of Allahabad Allahabad.
25. Verma, Dr. Surendra. (1978) "Modern Search for Peace", In *Journal of Gandhian Studies*, Vol. 5 No. 21, October.
26. Quartey, Francis Ofosu. "Gandhian Concept of Non-Violence", In *Journal of Gandhian Studies*, Vol. 7 No. 28 July 1980 Gandhi Bhawan, University of Allahabad.

Bibliography

Arora Ramesh, K. and Rajni Goyal (1996). *Indian Public Administration Institutions and Issues*, 2nd edition, New Delhi: Wishwa Prakashan.

Adams Guy and Danny, L. Balfour (1984). "Ethical Failing, Incompetence and Administrative Evil (lessons from Kartina and Iraq)", In *Ethics and Integrity in Public Administration: Concepts and Cases*, edited by Raymond W. Cox III, New York : M.E. Sharpe.

Agarwal (1986). *Constitutional Development of India and National Movement*, Delhi: S. Chand and Company.

Aung San Suu Kyi (1991) "Winer of Nobel Peace Prize", (2002). *Human Development Report 2002*, page, 51, box 2.1, published for the United Nations Development Programme (UNDP). New York, Oxford, Oxford University Press.

Bharatiya, L.K. (1987). "Prospect of Change in Gandhian Lines", in *Journal of Gandhian Studies*, Gandhi Bhawan, University of Allahabad Allahabad.

Baxi (1994). *Human Rights and Human Wrongs*, New Delhi: Har Anand Publications.

Bhelkey, S.E (2002). "Inadequacy of Democracy", In *Governance and Human Rights*, edited by Bharat Jhunjhunwala, Kalpaz Publications.

Bhattacharya, Mohit (1987). *Public Administration*, Kolkata: The World Press Private Ltd.

Boorstin, Daniel J. (1974). *Democracy and Its Discontents*, New York: Random House.

Buggi, Chandra Sekhar (1978). "Relevance of Gandhian Political Ideas Today", In the *Journal of Gandhian Studies*, Volume 5. No. 18, January, Gandhi Bhawan, University of Allahabad: Institute of Gandhian Thought and Peace Studies.

Canley, Simon and Peter Jones (ed.) (1945). *Human Rights and Global Diversity*, London: Frank Cass.

Chatterjee, Dilip K. (1979). "Relevance of Satyagraha as a Technique of Conflict Resolution," In the *Journal of Gandhian Studies*, April, Vol. 6. No. 23.

Das, D. (2013). "Environmental Ethics Matter to Philosophy?", In *Manavayatam*, Vol. II. No. II, January, - June.

Denhardt, Robert B. (1990). "Public Administration Theory: the State of the Discipline", In *Public Administration (State of the Discipline)* edited by Naomi B. Lynn and Aaron Wildavsky, New Delhi: East-West Electric Press Pvt. Limited.

Dennis F. Thompson (1983). "Bureaucracy and Democracy", In *Democratic Theory and Practice*, (ed.) G. Duncan, Cambridge University Press, referred by Robert B. Denhardt: Public Administration Theory: the State of the Discipline, In *Public Administration (State of the Discipline)* edited by Naomi B. Lynn and Aaron Wildavsky, New Delhi: East-West Electric Press Pvt. Limited.

Doctor, Adi (1997). *Political Thinkers of Modern India*, New Delhi : Mittal Publications.

Dubhasi, P.R. (2016). *Administrative Reforms*, Delhi: B.R. Publishing Corporation.

Ebadi, Shirin; "Globalization and Cultural Choice," chapter 5, Human Development Report 2004, (UNDP).

Gandhi: *Young India*, 13th November 1924.

Gandhi: *Harijan*, 5th May 1946.

Goel, Aruna and S.L. Goel (2005). *Human Values and Education*. New Delhi: Deep & Deep Publications Pvt. Ltd.

Grover, Dr. D.C. (1977) *Satyagraha: An Answer to International Conflict*, Institute of Gandhian Thought and Peace, Gandhi Bhawan, University of Allahabad, Vol. 4 No. 16. July.

Haldipur, R.N.: The Citizen, Society and Decision-making", In *IJPA*, Spl. issue On Citizen-Administration- I July –September Vol. XXI No. 3.

Hazarika, N. (2012). "Ethical Vacuity in Administration", In *Democratic Administration for Good Governance*, New Delhi: Kanishka.

Hoseah, Edward G (2014). "Corruption as a global hindrance to promoting ethics, integrity, and sustainable development in Tanzania: the role of the anti-corruption agency" published online: 4th November 2014, (Edward G. Hoseahis the Director General of Prevention and Combating of Corruption Board in Tanzania and is a member of the Tanzania Bar Association. He was the first President of the Eastern Africa Association of Anti-Corruption Authorities. He also served as a Chairman of the Southern African Forum Against Corruption and the African Union Advisory Boar on Corruption. He is currently Vice President of International Association of Anti-Corruption Authorties and is also a Board member of the International Society for the Reform of Criminal Law).

Jain, R.B. and Jashree Pillai (1985). "Transplanting Ombudsman in India", In *The Indian Journal of Public Administration*, July-September, Vol. XXXI No. 3.

Jain. R.B. (2013). "Reinventing Good Governance: Challenges and Strategies in India", In *Governance and Society*, edited by Neelam Trivedi and others, New Delhi: Rawat Publications.

James C. Worthy and James. C. (1959). *Big Business and Free Men*, New York: Harper.

Iyer, V.R. Krishna (1980). *Justice and Beyond*, Rajouri Garden, New Delhi: Deep and Deep Publications.

Kantowsky, Deltlef, University of Konstanz, Germany (West) paper contributed to: "Modern Search for Peace: The Gandhian Way" Conference of the Indian Society of Gandhian Studies.

Kapur, A.C. (2003). *Principles of Political Science*, New Delhi: S. Chand & Company.

Khatami, Seyed Mohmmad, President of the Islamic Republic of Iran: Human Development Report 2002, published for the United Nations Development Programme (UNDP), New York' Oxford, Oxford University Press.

Kennedy, John. F. (1956), *Profiles in Courage*. Text compilation by Ombica Gupta, by Kanti Roy, Sikandra Road, New Delhi: William D. Miller for the United States Information Service.

Kofi Annan (2002). *United Nations Development Programme (UNDP)*. New York' Oxford, Oxford University Press.

Lawton, Alan and Michael Macaulay (2009). "Ethics Management and Ethical Management", In *Ethics and Integrity in Public Administration, Concepts and Cases*, edited by Raymond W. Cox III, M.E. Sharpe, Inc.

Maheswari, S.R. (1988). *Indian Administration*, New Delhi: Orient Longman Private Ltd.

Malhorta, Dr. S.L. and Dr. S.K. Sharma, Research Monograph, Towards Village Swaraj, January 1977, Department of Gandhian Studies, Panjab University, Chandigarh.

McGregor (1960). *The Human Side of Enterprise*, New York, McGraw-Hill.

Misra, R.K. (1957). *Political Legacy of Plato and Aristotle*, Allahabad: Kitab Mahal.

Mohnot, S.R. (2007). "Relevance of Hindu Philosophy to Understand India", In *Understanding India* edited by Subhash Chandra Kashyap and Abhaya Kashayap, New Delhi: Vitasta Pubishing Ltd.

Munirathnam, K. (1987) "Relevance of Gandhian Conception of Freedom to Present Society", In *Journal of Gandhian Studies*, Vol. 14, No. 54-55, January-April 1987. Institute of Gandhian Thought & Peace Studies, Gandhi Bhawan, University of Allahabad, Allahabad.

Mukhopadhyay, Lipi (2002). "Social Conditioning and Deviant Behaviour," *IIPJ*, Spl. No. Social Tensions, July-Sept 2002 Vol. XLVIII, No. 3.

Naseema, C. (2002). *Human Rights Education: Conceptual and Pedagological Aspects*, New Delhi: Kanishka Publisher & Distributors.

Palkhiwala, Nani. (1997). *We, The People*, (11th print 1997)Delhi: UBS Publisher and Distributors Ltd.

Prasad, V.S., P. Satyanarayana and Y. Pardhasaradhi (2011). *Administrative Thinkers*, New Delhi: Sterling Publishers.

Quartey, Francis Ofosu. "Gandhian Concept of Non-violence", In *Journal of Gandhian Studies*, Vol. 7 No. 28 July 1980, Gandhi Bhawan, University of Allahabad, Allahabad.

Radhakrishnan, S. (1970). *The Present Crisis of Faith*, Delhi: Orient.

Radhakrishnan, S. (1961). *Recovery of Faith*, George Allen and Unwin Ltd. References.

Rao, V. Venkata (1980). *History of Political Theories*, New Delhi: S. Chand and Company.

Rao, K.L. Seshagiri, (1978) "Non-Violence and Peace", In the *Journal of Gandhian Studies*: Vol. 3 No. 21, October, University of Allahabad, Allahabad.

Rohr, John A.: *Ethics in Public Administration: A State-of-the-Discipline Report*, (ed.) Naomi B. Lynn and Aaron Wildavsky, New Delhi: East-West Electric Press Pvt. Limited.

Robertson, Ian (1980). *Sociology*, Worth Publishing, Inc.

Sharma, D.S. (1967). *Hinduism Through The Ages*, Bharatiya Vidya Bhawan, Chowpatty, Bombay.

Sharma, G. (1998). *Human Rights and Legal Remedies*, Deep and Deep Publication, New Delhi.

Sharma, Dr. M.P. and Dr. B.L. Sadana, (2004), *Public Administration in Theory and Practice*, Kitab Mahal, Sarojini Naidu Marg, Allahabad, 40th reprint).

Stahl, O.G. (1962). *Public Personnel Administration*, fifth edition, New Delhi: Oxford & IBH Publishing Co.

Singh, Ashok (1984), "Power of Non-Violence: Gandhian Concept," In the *Journal of Gandhian Studies*, Institute of Gandhian Thought and Peace Studies, Gandhi Bhawan, University of Allahabad, Vol. 11. No. 43-44, April/July.

Singh, Kh. Budhachandra (2011), Unpublished Ph.D. thesis on Gandhian Approach to Non-Violence and Peace, submitted to Manipur University.

Treadwell, Donald and Jill B. Treadwell (2005). *Public Relations Writing*, (second edition), New Delhi: Response Books, A Division of Sage Publications.

Tripathi, Anil (1980), "Gandhiji's Social Philosophy" In *Journal of Gandhian Stidies*, Vol. 7 No. 28 July, Gandhi Bhawan, University of Allahabad, Allahabad.

Tiwari, Kedarnath, *Comparative Religion*, Delhi: Motilal Bararassi Dass.

Tyagi, A.R. (1989). *Public Administration*, (6th revised edition), Delhi: Atma Ram & Sons.

Valsangkar, Krishna, Marina Pinto, Louis D'Silva: *Aspects of Political Theory*, Orienet Longman, Kolkata.

Verma, Dr. Surendra (1978), "Modern Search for Peace", In *Journal of Gandhian Studies*: Vol. 5 No. 21, October.

Report of the Santhanam Committee on Prevention of Corruption 1962.

The Chapter 2, Democratic Governance for Human Development, Human Development Report 2002, published for the United Nations Development Programme (UNDP), New York' Oxford, Oxford University Press 2002.

United Nations–Public Administration in the Second United Nations Development Decade: report of the Second Meeting of Experts (ST/TAO/M/57), 1971.

United Nations–Decentralization for National and Local Development Decade: Report of the Second Meeting of Experts (ST/TAO/M/19), 1971).

UN, 2001: World Public Sector Report: Globalization and the State, 2001, New Work.

World Commission on Culture and Development 1995, UN200a: Globalization and Cultural Choice, chapter 5, Box 5:2 Human Development Report 2004, published for UNDP.

World Medical Association' Medical Ethics Manual BP.63.01212 Femey-Voltaire Cedex, France. website. www wma.net.

cvc.nic.in/sites/default/files/ault/scr_rpt_cvc.pdf 4.8.2018.

economics.about.com/globalizationtrade/aaglobalization.htm

economics.about.com/globalizationtrade/aaglobalization.htm

economics.about.com/globalizationtrade/aaglobalization.htm)

economics.about.com/globalizationtrade/aaglobalization.htm)ww.fibre2fashion.com/industry-article/873

En.wikipedia.org/Moral_responsibility: accessed on 17.6.2014

En.wikipedia.org/Moral_responsibility: accessed on 17.6.2018

en.wikipedia.org/wiki/Human Rights

file:/A/Node002/network%209famyo/human%20Rights%20t Teaching htm.26.5.2018

http://en.wikipedia.org/wiki/philosophy, 19.4.2018

http://en.wikipedia.org/wiki/philosophy, 19.4.2018

http://en.wikipedia.org/wiki/Rule_of_law 6.12.2014

http://en.wikipedia.org/wiki/Rule_of_law 6.12.2014

http://www.preservearticles.com/2012031427266/what-are-the-causes-of-administrative-corruption-in-india.htmlAccessed on 27.6.2018

http://www.un.org/events/non-violenceday/ accessed 25th March 2019

https://currentaffairs.gktoday.intags/international-day-of-non-vilence, accessed on 25th March 2019

https://en.wikipedia.or/wiki/Good_governance 25.1.2018

https://en.wikipedia.or/wiki/Good_governance 25.1.2018

https://en.wikipedia.org/wiki/corruption_in_India dt 25/12/218.

https://en.wikipedia.org/wiki/OECD_Anti-Bribery_Convention dt 4.1.2019

https://en.wikipedia.org/wiki/Prevention_of_Corruption_Act_1988, dt. 3.10.2018. (https://www.linkedin.com/pulse/what-professionalism-does-mean-you-daniel-w-porcupile, 4.18.2018) https://en.wikipedia.org/wiki/the_Lokpal_and_Lokayukta_act_2013 accessed on 4.6.2018

https://en.wikipedia.org/wikiCorruption_in_India. Accessed on 24.5.2018.

https://en.wikipedia.org/wikiCorruption_in_India. Accessed on 24.5.2018.

https://internatinal day of peace.org/get-involved/nonviolence/ accessed on 25th March 2019

https://news.un.org/en./story/2007/06/222502-un-declares-2-october-gandhis-birthday-international-day-non-violence accessed 0n 25th March 2019

https://times of India.indiatimes.com/india/6-years-after-signig-india-yet-to-ratify-UN-Conv. Date 18.6.2018

https://www.civilservicein india.com/subject/corruption-in-india 1html dt 24.12.2018

https://www.civilserviceindia.com/subject/essay/ana-hazare-movement-against-corruption%20%html 1.4.2019

https://www.civilserviceindia.com/subject/essay/corruption-in-india.html, accessed on 18.6.2018.

https://www.daysoftheyear.com/days/international-day-of-non-violence accessed on 25th March 2019

https://www.google.com/search?q=Speech+by=Wolfensohn+Cancer+of+corruption& rlz=kicHBD.enINBIINB dt.21/1/2019.

https://www.google.com/search?q=united=nations+convention+against+corruption&riz=ICICIN8IIIN8II dt 11.1.2029

https://www.invstopedia.com/terms/o/oecd.asp dated 29.6.2018

https://www.linkedin.com/pulse/what-professionalism-does-mean-you-daniel-w-porcupile, 4.8.2018

https://www.nelsonmandela.org/content/page/biography, dt.21/12/2018

https://www.nvestpedia.com/terms/o/oecd.asp dt.29.6.2018.

https://www.oecd.org/daf/anti-bribery_recommendation_brief.pdf. dt 6.1.2019.

https://www.tandfonline.com/doi/full/10.1080/17449626.2014.973995

https://www.un.org/en/events/nonviolenceday/background.shtml accessed on 25th March 2019

https://www.unodc.org/southasis/enfrontpage/2011.may/indian-govt-ratifies-two-un-conventions.html date 18.6.2018.

Indiaprosppect.org/Blog/?23 1st Apl. 2019

unpan/un.org/intradoc/groups/public/documents/un-padm/unpan049589-pdf 30.6.2018

www.businessdictionary.com/definition/globalization.html).

www.fibre2fashion.com/industry-article/8738/ompact-of-globalization1.asp

www.mildredwarner-org/govt-restructuring/re-inventing-govt

www.mildredwarner-org/govt-restructuring/re-inventing-govt

www.mildredwarner-org/govt-restructuring/re-inventing-govt.www.unpan.org/DPADM/Events/GlobalForumReinventing government/tabid/441/language/en-US/default.aspx

www.mildredwarner-org/govt-restructuring/re-inventing-govt.www.unpan.org/DPADM/Events/GlobalForumReinventing government/tabid/441/language/en-US/default.aspx
www.ohchr.org/en/issues/pages/whatarehuman rights.asp
www.unescap.org/pdd/prs/ProjectActivities/Ongoing/gg/governance/.asp
www.unescap.org/pdd/prs/ProjectActivities/Ongoing/gg/governance/.asp

Index